"I always love Greg Ogden's work! He consistently calls us back to the core practice of the church—making disciples. And here he gives us a proven process that is intensely relational, thoroughly biblical and readily accessible to serious disciplemakers."

Bill Donahue, Executive Director, Small Group Ministries,
Willow Creek Association

"Greg Ogden presents a model for discipleship that really works. We have also discovered the life-changing dynamic found in groups of three. I enthusiastically recommend that you prayerfully apply the principles shared from the crucible of experience. Transformation awaits!"

Bob Logan, CoachNet International Ministries

"Greg Ogden draws on his extensive pastoral experience as well as his interaction with many pastors in the Fuller D.Min. classes to provide an extensive range of biblical principles and practical ministry insights. He establishes the foundations for a reproducible model of discipleship. The issue is urgent and widespread in the churches of North America. This is the kind of book to help make a significant difference."

Eddie Gibbs, Donald A. McGavran Professor of Church Growth,
Fuller Theological Seminary, and author of ChurchNext

"People are built to last. So why is the church still keeping score on its institutional successes rather than tracking the development of disciples? Greg Ogden's insightful suggestions can help a church redesign its scorecard to celebrate transformed lives."

Reggie McNeal, Director of Leadership Development,
South Carolina Baptist Convention

"After reading *Transforming Discipleship*, the reader is likely to exclaim, 'I can do that!' Greg Ogden has cut through the cultural and ministerial fog surrounding this subject and written a persuasive handbook on the priority and process of this essential element. Readers will also recognize this book as eminently practical with helpful explanations of 'whys' and facilitating steps for 'hows.' Greg has convincingly urged the absolute priority of this focus on transformation in the making of a people who will carry the mission and message to the next generation. And you can join him in doing that!"

Julie Gorman, Professor of Christian Formation and Discipleship, Fuller Theological Seminary

"Greg Ogden supplied us a comprehensive, biblical curriculum in *Discipleship Essentials*. In *Transforming Discipleship* he reveals the foundation and vision. Based on a creative and stimulating triad model, Greg provides a vehicle that will guide the training of leaders who in turn will equip the church and individuals for a life of transformational discipleship. In a refreshingly biblical and realistic manner, Greg sculpts an essential model that goes beyond programs to the intentional development of relationships that are empowered by the Spirit to grow together to become like Jesus."

Michael J. Wilkins, Dean of the Faculty, Talbot School of Theology, Biola University, and author of Following the Master: A Biblical Theology of Discipleship

"Greg Ogden's credentials as a local church pastor give him both the credibility and the courage to speak a bold, hard truth with a soft clarity: that leaders (by their behavior) have lost sight of the call of the church to go and make disciples. More important, he creates a road map for the process. *Transforming Discipleship* is a transferable training model, based on Jesus' and Paul's unique and similar adaptive styles of leadership and empowerment, that is so simple it is brilliant. *Transforming Discipleship* is a call to action for all church leaders seeking to honor and embody the Great Commission."

Sue Mallory, author of The Equipping Church: Serving Together to Transform Lives

"Greg Ogden has a heart for making disciples. He lives it. He speaks it. He writes it. This book is the mind of Greg's heart and, I believe, is a reflection of Jesus' heart and mind. Jesus wants his church to make disciples in a post-Christian world. This book puts the ministry leader and visionary in touch with today's stark reality—it's time for the whole church to get serious about making disciples Jesus' way. This book will help change our church to be in alignment with Jesus' vision and ministry practice."

Gareth Icenogle, Senior Pastor, First Presbyterian Church, Bethlehem, Pennsylvania, and author of The Biblical Foundations of Small Group Ministry

"Greg Ogden's first book, *The New Reformation*, has had a profound influence on my work. And in *Transforming Discipleship*, Ogden describes the next stage in American Christianity, the change of emphasis from proclamation to demonstration, with great force and clarity. This is a truly important book."

Bob Buford, Founder and Chairman, Leadership Network, and author of Halftime: Changing Your Game Plan from Success to Significance

"While *Transforming Discipleship* is packed full with good, useful, biblical insights, the two unique features that especially connect with discipleship in a postmodern world are the concepts of triad discipleship and the shift from the hierarchical and authoritative models that dominated discipleship in modernity to 'discipling as a mutual process of peer mentoring.' This work is more biblical and more compelling than anything I have seen to date."

Robert Webber, Myers Professor of Ministry, Northern Baptist Theological Seminary

"Why are Christians not more like Christ? With all the evangelism, church growth and discipleship programs, both critics and lovers of the church around the world ask, where are the transformed lives? Greg Ogden does not claim all the answers. He does point out one important truth: transformation happens not through programs but through highly accountable, mutually encouraging, Spirit-formed relationships. All those concerned about a 'disciple deficit' will find this not only a must-read but a must-practice book!"

Leighton Ford, President, Leighton Ford Ministries

TRANSFORMING
DISCIPLESHIP

Making

Disciples

a Few at

a Time

GREG OGDEN

InterVarsity Press
Downers Grove, Illinois

InterVarsity Press
P.O. Box 1400, Downers Grove, IL 60515-1426
World Wide Web: www.ivpress.com
E-mail: mail@ivpress.com

InterVarsity Press® is the book-publishing division of InterVarsity Christian Fellowship/USA®, a student
movement active on campus at hundreds of universities, colleges and schools of nursing in the United States of
America, and a member movement of the International Fellowship of Evangelical Students. For information
about local and regional activities, write Public Relations Dept., InterVarsity Christian Fellowship/USA, 6400
Schroeder Rd., P.O. Box 7895, Madison, WI 53707-7895, or visit the IVCF website at <www.ivcf.org>.

Cover design: Cindy Kiple

Cover and interior images: Eyewire Collection/Getty Images

ISBN 0-8308-2388-3

Printed in the United States of America ∞

Library of Congress Cataloging-in-Publication Data

Ogden, Greg.
    Transforming discipleship: making disciples a few at a time / Greg
Ogden.
       p. cm.
Includes bibliographical references.
    ISBN 0-8308-2388-3 (pbk.: alk. paper)
    1. Discipling (Christianity) I. Title.
    BV4520.O033 2003
    253—dc21
                                                                                                          2003001547

| P | 17 | 16 | 15 | 14 | 13 | 12 | 11 | 10 | 9 | 8 | 7 | 6 | 5 | 4 | 3 | 2 | 1 |
| Y | 15 | 14 | 13 | 12 | 11 | 10 | 09 | 08 | 07 | 06 | 05 | 04 | 03 | | | | |

CONTENTS

INTRODUCTION

A Story of Transformation

I admit I stumbled onto a discovery, yet it has become one of the most amazing ahas of my pastoral ministry. This discovery was the result of an experiment. I had written a first draft of a discipleship curriculum, which turned into the final project for my doctor of ministry degree.[1] The focus of the project was to implement this curriculum in the local church and then to evaluate its effectiveness. Up to this point in my ministry, I had equated making disciples with a one-to-one relationship. After all, wasn't the Paul-Timothy model the definition of discipling? The point was to grow a disciple who would make a disciple, and so on.

My adviser in the doctoral program suggested that I consider a variety of contexts in which I could test the curriculum and then track the dynamics of a discipling relationship. One of the options I chose was to invite two other people to join me on the journey to maturity in Christ. I did not anticipate the potency that would be unleashed in what I have since come to call a triad. It would forever change my understanding of the means that the Holy Spirit uses to transform people into Christ's image.

ERIC'S STORY OF TRANSFORMATION

To illustrate the power of a triad, I will tell the story of Eric's transformation. Eric was one of my first two recruits on this discipleship adventure, and he had approached me stating his interest in a mentoring relationship. Eric's spiritual ambivalence at the time may not have made him the best candidate for an intensive investment. He was just two years out of college. Looking like a fashion model who had walked straight out of the pages of a men's clothing catalog, Eric was the envy of his male friends. Because of his chiseled good looks, attracting women was the least of his problems. He was making more money than he had ever dreamed possible. He had a promising future with his new company. All of this was alluring to him.

In spite of the world's draw, Eric also had a strong pull toward following Christ. It was a matter of who would win the tug of war—Jesus or the world. I mentioned to Eric that I had written a new curriculum and was eager to have some people try it. I made sure that he knew that to be involved in this relationship would require an intense investment: a topical study of Scripture and its application to daily life, memorization of Bible verses, and transparent interaction with me and one other person. The high bar was set, yet Eric said he was willing to give it a go.

A restaurant located equidistant between our work places became the place where we were joined by Karl, who at the time was an administrator of an engineering firm. Over lunch we laid our open Bibles and study materials on the restaurant table and proceeded to interact over the content. What impressed me was the energetic interchange in our conversation. Something about adding a third party to the one-on-one made our conversation come alive. Even though I was the only pastor among the three, I didn't sense that I had to be the focal point or the ever-flowing fountain of wisdom. Our relationship turned into a peer discipling one in which each of us could honestly share our insights into the Word and its application to our situations.

Eric was quite open about his divided heart. The enticement of a life of comfort and serial female relationships seemed tempting. He told us about making eye contact with an attractive female motorist while driving through Los Angeles traffic. The next thing he knew, they had pulled off on a side street to exchange phone numbers. Karl and I listened to the story with more than a bit of envy, without any comparable stories to tell. Yet we also understood how seductive sexual power could be for Eric. It was creating a fissure in his heart.

Still, Eric could not get away from the magnetic appeal of Jesus Christ. There was something about the power of the person of Jesus and the life of adventure to which he has called us that would not allow Eric to shake him off. In our second lesson we explored Jesus' normative standard for all who would follow him. Jesus said, "If any want to become my followers, let them deny themselves and take up their cross daily and follow me. For those who want to save their life will lose it, and those who lose their life for my sake will save it" (Luke 9:23-24). Eric was faced with the same choice Moses posed to the people of Israel: "See, I have set before you today life and prosperity, death and adversity. . . . Choose life" (Deuteronomy 30:15, 19).

It was not too many weeks into our time together when Eric announced that he was going to quit his job and see the world. He wanted to take the better part of a year for a freelance exploration of this planet. In his young, carefree and unattached years, he desired to do what he might not be able to do later when more responsibilities would weigh on him. He reasoned that he could always get a job when he returned, but this stage of his life would come only once. This decision precipitated some forthright comments. It was evident that Eric was drifting into a life of self-absorption. Searching for a way to speak to this carefree attitude, I said, "Eric, at least consider taking a month or two of this time to invest somewhere in a mission opportunity. Pause long enough to immerse yourself in God's work in your travels and rub shoulders with quality Christian people who are giving themselves away for the sake of the gospel."

I don't remember the exact sequence of events or steps in the shift, but before I knew it, Eric decided to abandon his vagabond plans. He signed on for a summer mission opportunity with Campus Crusade for Christ in Hungary and Poland. This was prior to the fall of communism in Eastern Europe. I have often reflected on the power of being able to speak a word of truth or challenge into a life. If we had not had the regularity of relationship and the trust that had been built in those few months, I doubt that Eric would have had a context in which to hear a confrontive word that had the potential to redirect his life.

When Eric returned that summer from his adventures, he was a transformed individual. The divided heart had become singularly subsumed under the lordship of Jesus. Eric regaled us with stories of sharing the gospel on the lakeside beaches of Hungary and stealthy forays into Poland. People were hungry for the good news, and he saw Jesus Christ grab hold of and redirect lives, not the least of which was his own.

Upon his return, Eric immediately went onto Campus Crusade staff with the intent of taking business people into the eastern-bloc countries in order to crack open their hearts to the work of the life-changing gospel in these barricaded regions. At the same time he reconnected with a high school sweetheart, who also was a passionate follower of Jesus. It seemed only a matter of months before they were engaged and Betsy was ready to join Eric on staff with Campus Crusade. These two lit up rooms with their radiant joy in service to Christ and their love for each other. They honored me by asking if I would perform their wedding in Portland, Oregon, alongside Betsy's pastor.

A number of weeks prior to the wedding, Eric was experiencing debilitating back pain that he assumed was caused by a recent motorcycle accident. Even with physical therapy, however, he was showing no improvement. On the Monday prior to their Saturday wedding, a tumor was discovered pressing up against Eric's spine. Testicular cancer had spread to multiple parts of his body. The prognosis was not good. He was admitted to the hospital that day and began a heavy regimen of chemotherapy.

Eric and Betsy's spirits were undaunted. The wedding would go on, but there needed to be a quick change of venue. The church wedding was replaced by the hospital chapel, which could hold a standing-room-only crowd. The scene was something out of a made-for-TV movie that was designed to manipulate emotions. But this was real life. Eric's hospital bed was rolled into chapel with Eric inclined at almost a ninety-degree angle. The bed covers came up to his waist, with his upper torso appropriately dressed in his tuxedo. Betsy, his bride, stood bedside, holding Eric's hand in her right hand and her bouquet in the other. The wedding party flanked the bed on either side. There is usually considerable anticipation at weddings, but rarely is the air as thick with lump-in-the-throat emotions as it was in this packed chapel. Seventeen years after this event, I have no trouble remembering the thickness in my windpipe and the struggle to focus on my notes through my blurry and misty eyes.

In the ensuing months, the chemotherapy took a toll on this handsome man. On his better days, Eric was able to travel. I still have vivid images of him walking into our Southern California church with his knit cap covering his billiard-ball head and looking very gaunt. Yet his spirit was undaunted. He radiated the indwelling presence of Jesus Christ. I knew that this was a man living the words of the apostle Paul, "So we do not lose heart. Even though our outer nature is wasting away, our inner nature is being renewed day by day" (2 Corinthians 4:16).

When Eric had to go back into the hospital for further treatments, I flew to Oregon to visit him. As I was walking toward Eric's hospital room, some of his buddies from high school were leaving. These young men, who could normally make light of anything, were unusually sullen. They said to me, "You know what Eric said?

He said that cancer is the best thing that ever happened to him. Can you believe that?" Eric obviously would have preferred it otherwise, but he had come to cast his entire hope upon Jesus Christ, and his Lord and Lover had not let him down.

Eric said of his discoveries, "God is helping me grow closer to him. It [the cancer] has made me realize whom I have to depend on. And I have seen through these experiences that when I do call upon God that he really helps in his way. It may not mean that he will relieve the pain or that he will cure the cancer immediately. It may mean that I die, or live . . . that does not matter. What is important is that I keep my eyes on him.

"One morning a doctor came in when Betsy was with me and said, 'I want to tell you the X-rays are not very encouraging. You may want to consider getting things in order and stopping treatment.' This was the first time it occurred to me that I might die. I might not live through this.

"It really caused me to reassess what I am placing my faith in. Am I placing my faith in the doctors and drugs, or am I placing my faith in God? If I am placing my faith in God, I have the assurance that he will deliver me out of the situation I am in. . . . It may not mean that he will cure the cancer or that I will survive. . . . But that is not what is important. It goes back to keeping my eyes on him."

Seven months after his marriage to Betsy, Eric died on April 25, 1986, at the age of twenty-five. Here was a man who in a short time went from ambivalence about following Jesus Christ to wholehearted trust and devotion.

OUR JOURNEY OF TRANSFORMATION

I introduce this book with Eric's story, for in essence the change in Eric is what this book is about, and that is the process and context for transformation into Christlikeness. What I stumbled into with Eric and Karl opened up for me an exploratory journey into the optimum settings and ingredients necessary to create the conditions for being conformed to the image of Christ. Since this initial experience I have repeatedly witnessed the power of triads. Triads provide the setting to bring together the necessary elements for transformation or growth to maturity in Christ. What have I observed in this setting?

- Multiplication or reproduction: empowering those who are discipled to disciple others

- Intimate relationships: developing deep trust as the soil for life change

- Accountability: lovingly speaking truth into another's life

- Incorporation of the biblical message: covering the themes of Scripture sequentially to create a holistic picture of the Christian life

- Spiritual disciplines: practicing the habits that lead to intimacy with Christ and service to others

This book will introduce to you a missing tool in the arsenal of disciple making that will lead to life-transforming experiences such as Eric's. For the better part of two decades I have had at least one triad as a part of my weekly schedule. Never do I feel more fulfilled as a pastor than when I am sharing my life with two others who are on an intentional journey to maturity in Christ. Then to see these same partners empowered to disciple others so that multiple generations of Christians are firmly rooted and reproduce . . . that is about as good as it gets!

I am excited about the discoveries that lie ahead for you. In the ensuing pages you will learn a simple, reproducible approach to making disciples. This approach is grounded in the biblical model of Jesus and Paul, who intentionally grew followers into responsible, reproducing disciples and disciple makers.

In chapters one and two, we will examine the urgency of this issue. Bill Hull has prophetically written, "The crisis at the heart of the church is a crisis of product."[2] Disciple making, discipleship and discipling are hot topics today, because we see such a great need for this focus in our churches. I recently cotaught a first-time course in a doctor of ministry program titled "Growing a Disciple-Making Congregation." Usually it takes new classes some time to catch on, because students don't want to be lab rats in new course development. They wait to hear from others how it went. Not so with this class. We had one of our largest classes during my tenure as head of this program. Why? There is an evident discipleship deficit in our churches and ministries that we know needs to be addressed, but we are not sure how to do so.

Chapter one will examine the symptoms of the deficit of disciples, while chapter two will attempt to unearth the root causes of these symptoms. The intent of this rather sobering discussion is not to air the church's dirty laundry or condemn Christian leaders. Who needs self-flagellation? Yet the first step toward recovering Jesus' mission statement for the church, "Go and make disciples," is to evaluate the extent of the need. A sober assessment of the gap between Jesus' stated end and our practice will define the cost for completing the task. Chapters one and two will provide tools for you to assess the symptoms and causes of the discipleship deficit in your church or ministry.

In chapters three through five, we will explore Jesus' and Paul's approaches to making disciples as a basis for our disciple making. In spite of highly readable and insightful works on Jesus' and Paul's strategies of growing followers,[3] Christian leaders do not seem to translate this into workable ministry practice. In all of my teaching through seminars and courses on making disciples Jesus' way, I still sense that a very small percentage of pastors and church leaders emulate Jesus' and Paul's models. So it is worth asking again, How did transformation take place in those who traveled with Jesus and Paul on their itinerant ministry? Jesus staked the future of his ministry on his investment in a few. Do we do the same? Why did Jesus choose the Twelve and spend so much of his time with them? If we were to follow this model, what would it look like? Why is it that we can name those who were trainees and partners in Paul's ministry? What does this say about the way we should carry out our ministry? When we can make evident connections between the scriptural models and our ministry practice, the people of God understand in a powerful way.

Once the biblical model of Jesus and Paul has refreshed our theological vision, we will see how the imperative to make disciples a few at a time can be become integral to our church- or ministry-based approach. Chapters six through eight will examine three of the critical issues that need to be addressed in any disciple-making strategy. First, disciple making is about relational investment. It is walking alongside a few invited fellow travelers in an intentional relationship over time. You will hear this constant refrain: Disciple making is not a program but a relationship.

Second, we rightly associate disciple making with multiplication. Yet the promise always seems to far exceed the results. Discipleship programs are sold to us with the promise that disciples will be multiplied through intergenerational transference from life to life. The reality is that we rarely get beyond the first generation. Yet we have not made disciples if we only help people grow to maturity without also seeing them reproduce. I have lived the frustration of not seeing those in whom I have invested go on to disciple others. I have also witnessed some wonderful breakthroughs of empowerment. I am eager to share these discoveries with you.

Third, making disciples is a transformative process. I will identify the convergence of the key ingredients that make transformation of a life by the Holy Spirit possible, as in Eric's case. What ingredients placed Eric's life in the transformative laboratory of the Holy Spirit? When we bring together transparent relationships and the truth of God's Word in the context of covenantal accountability for life change, then we have stepped into the Holy Spirit's sweet spot that makes life change possible.

The three elements of relational investment, multiplication and transformation come together powerfully in the model of reproducible triads.

In chapter nine we will look at the steps necessary for a church- or ministry-based discipling strategy. We will address practical questions: What is a workable disciple-making model? Whom should we invite into the discipling process? How do we get started? How can we grow a multigenerational network of disciples? How do we keep up the motivation for multiplication through the generations?

Some of you don't need to be convinced that there is a disciple deficit in your churches, nor do you need to revisit the biblical vision for how disciples are made. You are looking for a practical strategy to make it happen. I will not be offended if you leap over the first part of the book and go directly to the last part, which is designed to assist you in practical implementation of a disciple-making strategy.

Since first stumbling on the power of triads with Eric and Karl almost two decades ago, I have had the privilege to walk with many others in this life-altering relationship and observe the growth of multigenerational discipling networks in two churches. Over this period I have heard from people across North America and around the world whose lives and ministries have been radically changed because they employed multiplying triads. What encourages me in the enormous discipleship challenge facing the church is that there is less of a want-to than there is a need for how-to. When the urgency for disciple making can be fanned by the vision of the biblical pattern of investing in a few at a time and then translated into a practical strategy, there is the hope that we can truly fulfill Jesus' mission statement for everyone of his church, "Go therefore and make disciples of all nations" (Matthew 28:19).

PART ONE

The Discipleship Deficit

What Went Wrong and Why

1

THE DISCIPLESHIP GAP
Where Have All the Disciples Gone?

If we are to devise a successful strategy of disciple making in our churches, we must first assess the gap between where we are and where we are called to go. Jesus promoted this approach when he challenged those who would follow him to first count the cost. "For which of you, intending to build a tower, does not first sit down and estimate the cost, to see whether you have enough to complete it?" (Luke 14:28).

Max De Pree, who has popularized this biblical wisdom as top priority for leaders, writes, "The first responsibility of a leader is to define reality."[1] Why is it important to define reality? If we are trying to go somewhere, we first must know where we are in relationship to where we want to go. For example, when we are trying to find a particular store in a shopping mall, the first thing we do is locate the directory that displays the floor plan of all the shops. Our eyes immediately land on the red dot with an arrow pointing to it that says, "You are here!" Once we know where we are, we can locate our intended destination and plot the pathway to get there.

In the remainder of this chapter we will explore the deficit that must be filled if making self-initiating, reproducing, fully devoted followers of Christ is to become our new reality. In the next chapter the picture of current reality will be completed by looking at the causes of how we got to where we are now. Only as we have a clear description of the problem and its roots can we suggest the solution.

The analysis in this chapter will assist you to assess the gap between where you are and where you want to go. A sober analysis of our ministry is hard work and takes considerable courage. The doctor of ministry program that I directed requires that all incoming students take an assessment course to measure their personal and ministerial health. As we put this new program in place, a nagging doubt lurked in my mind. What if Christian leaders would rather avoid holding up a mirror before their lives and ministries and would prefer a distorted, more favorable false impression about themselves? On the whole we attracted increasing numbers of leaders who wanted to live in reality rather than in fantasy. As you read on, quietly pause and ask the Holy Spirit to allow you to receive the truth that will ultimately set you free.

THE STATE OF DISCIPLESHIP TODAY: YOU ARE HERE!

If I were to choose one word to summarize the state of discipleship today, that word would be *superficial*. There appears to be a general lack of comprehension among many who claim Jesus as Savior as to the implications of following him as Lord. The Joint Statement on Discipleship at the Eastbourne Consultation began with an acknowledgment of need: "As we face the new millennium, we acknowledge that the state of the Church is marked by growth without depth. Our zeal to go wider has not been matched by a commitment to go deeper."[2] John Stott has added his voice on this matter: "For many years, 25 or more, the church-growth school has been dominant. I rejoice in the statistics, but we must say it is growth without depth. I believe it was Chuck Colson who said the church is 3,000 miles wide and an inch deep. Many are babes in Christ."[3]

This superficiality comes into startling focus when we observe the incongruity between the numbers of people who profess faith in Jesus Christ and the lack of impact on the moral and spiritual climate of our times. During the decade of the 1990s, Christian pollster George Barna tracked the numbers of those who identified themselves as born-again Christians.[4] The percentages of adults during the decade of the 1990s who fit this description ranged from a low of 35 percent to a high of 43 percent.[5] Barna's counterpart in the wider culture, George Gallup, asked whether people would describe themselves as "born again or evangelical." Over the same period an astonishing range of 35 to 49 percent so identified themselves.[6] These numbers scream for an explanation. How can Christian leaders moan over the moral decline of our society while so many people have indicated a meaningful encounter with Jesus Christ? If these multiple millions of Jesus' namers were Jesus' followers, we would not be wagging our fingers in shame at a civilization that has turned away from God.

Cal Thomas, a Christian syndicated columnist and social commentator, calls Christians to look at the quality of our discipleship instead of directing our indignation at the moral decay. He writes, "The problem in our culture . . . isn't the abortionists. It isn't the pornographers or drug dealers or criminals. It is the undisciplined, undiscipled, disobedient, and Biblically ignorant Church of Jesus Christ."[7]

How deep is the discipleship deficit that we face? What are the symptoms of superficiality that we witness in the church? We are able to gauge the discipleship deficit when we compare the biblical standards of discipleship with the reality of their achievement in our churches and ministries. What is the gap we observe between the biblical standard and the reality in our Christian communities?

Seven marks of discipleship will be described in the rest of this chapter. At the end of each section you will have an opportunity to identify the gap between the biblical standard and the reality of your ministry.

THE BIBLICAL STANDARD AND THE CURRENT REALITY

1. Proactive ministers. The Scriptures picture the church as full of proactive ministers; the reality is that a majority of church members are passive recipients.

The New Testament picture of the church is an every-member ministry. The "priesthood of all believers" is not just a Reformation watchword but also a radical biblical ideal. Writing to scattered, persecuted Christians, Peter refers to the church in aggregate when he writes, "You [plural] are . . . a royal priesthood" (1 Peter 2:9). Every believer comes to God via Christ as mediator, and every believer is enabled to act as a priest on behalf of fellow members of the body of Christ. Ministry that is biblically envisioned calls up images not of the paid priest who is set apart from and above the rest of the body of believers but of ordinary saints. The apostle Paul has the everyday Christian in mind when he writes, "To each is given the manifestation of the Spirit for the common good" (1 Corinthians 12:7). Playing off the image of the church as the body of Christ, Paul is saying that all believers have been given ministry gifts by the Holy Spirit and therefore each believer is equivalent to a body part that contributes to the health of the whole. The New Testament describes a full employment plan that dignifies and gives all believers value based on the contribution their gifts make in building up and extending the church.

Yet when we turn from the biblical standard of the first-century church to the reality of the church today, we see a relatively small percentage of people who move beyond Sunday worship into the life and ministry of a congregation or who experience ministry as a way of life. The 80/20 rule seems impossible to transcend. If we chart giving patterns, for example, 20 percent of a congregation gives 80 percent of the income. If we study the ministry profile of volunteers, we find that a fairly steady 20 percent serve the 80 percent who are consumers of their efforts.

Conversely, this means a high percentage of spectators are filling the pews. As a pastor, I was consciously aware that people arrived at worship with a reviewers' mentality. Worshipers see it as the responsibility of those on stage to provide an engaging, meaningful and entertaining show, while it is the worshipers' job to give an instant review of the worship service as they pass through the receiving line after worship. Doesn't it seem odd for people to make evaluative comments like "Good sermon, Pastor," or "I enjoyed the service this morning" about the worship of the living God? On many a Sunday after concluding the morning message, when I glanced in the direction of the choir I expected to see them raise cards from their laps rating the sermon—9.9, 9.4, and so on.

If ministry is largely being stewards of our spiritual gifts, then the task ahead is daunting. The good news is that Barna found that 85 percent of believers had heard of spiritual gifts. Of those 85 percent, however, half either were ignorant of the gifts they had or believed that God had bypassed them in the distribution process. One quarter of the people who thought they knew their spiritual gifts named gifts that had no correlation with a biblical profile. People said things like, "I have the gift of making cherry pies" or "I have the gift of gab." Only one quarter of the people who knew their spiritual gifts identified gifts that had a biblical basis.[8]

Rate your ministry on a scale of 1 to 5, with 1 being passive recipients and 5 being proactive ministers.		
DISCIPLESHIP SYMPTOM	RATING	NOTES
Passive recipients . . . Proactive ministers		

2. A disciplined way of life. The Scriptures picture followers of

Jesus as engaged in a disciplined way of life; the reality is that a small percentage of believers invests in spiritual growth practices.

Great and accomplished athletes perform effortlessly. What we don't see are the hours of repetitive practice that make Tiger Woods's golf swing look so smooth or Michael Jordan's last-second buzzer beater look routine. No matter how natural one's talent, the great athletes are great because they practice at a greater level than everyone else.

In the New Testament one of the consistent images for the Christian life is the discipline of an athlete. Comparing the Christian life with a race, Paul writes, "Athletes exercise self-control in all things; they do it to receive a perishable wreath, but we an imperishable one" (1 Corinthians 9:25). In making this comparison, Paul raises the bar. If athletes will put themselves through a rigorous regimen to get a "perishable wreath," how much more should Christians discipline themselves, because our goal is "an imperishable one"! The writer to the Hebrews urges believers to move beyond being milk-drinking infants to adult believers who can take in solid food. Using the image of the gymnasium and athletic exertion, he writes, "But solid food is for the mature, for those whose faculties have been trained by practice to distinguish good from evil" (Hebrews 5:14).[9] One is left with an obvious impression that leading the Christian life will require spiritual discipline. No accomplishment comes without practice and discipline.

Yet when we turn from the scriptural picture to today's church, we observe another version of the 80/20 rule. Studies have shown that only one out of six adults who attend Christian worship services is involved in a group or relational process designed to help them grow spiritually. Of the 17 percent involved in a corporate commitment, the means of choice by far is a small group (69 percent) that meets to study the Bible and consider the application of spiritual realities to life. Less common means of discipleship, in order of involvement, are an adult Sunday school class (20 percent), one-to-one mentoring (14 percent), a special faith-based class (11 percent) and online training or interaction geared to discipleship (3 percent).[10] Barna comments pointedly on his research, "In a society as fast-moving and complex as ours, people have to make choices every minute of the day. Unless people have a regular and focused exposure to the foundations of their faith, the chances of Christians consistently making choices to reflect biblical principles are minimal."[11]

When it comes to the personal or individual disciplines of the faith that would indicate an ordering of a person's life in relationship to Christ, the signs are no more hopeful. According to Barna, fewer than one in five born-again adults have any specific, measurable goals related to their spiritual development. In Barna's nationwide survey, interviews were conducted with hundreds of people, including pastors and church leaders, who regularly attended church services and programs. Barna concludes, "Not one of the adults we interviewed said that their goal in life was to be a committed follower of Jesus Christ or to make disciples of the entire world—or even their entire block."[12] When this group was asked what they wanted to accomplish in life, eight out of ten believers found success in family, career development and financial achievement. Dallas Willard concludes, "The fact is that there is now lacking a serious and expectant intention to bring Jesus' people into obedience and abundance through training."[13]

Rate your ministry on a scale of 1 to 5, with 1 being spiritually undisciplined and 5 being spiritually disciplined.		
DISCIPLESHIP SYMPTOM	RATING	NOTES
Spiritually undisciplined . . . Spiritually disciplined		

3. Discipleship affects all of life. The Scriptures picture discipleship as affecting all spheres of life; the reality is that many believers have relegated faith to the personal, private realm.

The dominant theme of Jesus' public ministry was the proclamation of the good news of the kingdom of God. The future, long-awaited kingdom, where the rule and reign of God would be actualized on earth, had broken into this present darkness in the person of the King, Jesus Christ. The promise is that those who "repent, and believe" the gospel (Mark 1:15) are transferred from the kingdom of darkness to the kingdom of the beloved Son (Colossians 1:13). A new authority or regime is established in the hearts of Jesus' followers. That authority affects all that we are in all that we do in all spheres of life. The motif of the kingdom means that there is not a scintilla of life that does not come under the authority of Jesus Christ. Fundamentally we are kingdom people, which means that Jesus is Lord in our hearts, homes and workplaces; our attitudes, thoughts and desires; our relationships and moral decisions; our political convictions and social conscience. In every area of our interior life, personal relationships or social involvement, we seek to know and live the mind and will of God.

Yet the reality is that we suffer today from the same bifurcated existence that Martin Luther addressed almost five hundred years ago with Reformation force. In writing his *Open Letter to the German Nobility,* Luther said that the first wall of Romanism was a false distinction between what he called the "spiritual estate" and "temporal estate."[14] In Luther's day the spiritual estate was the realm of the church and its holy orders, which took precedence over and elevated itself above the temporal estate, which was the realm of government and the common life. Luther attempted to break down the wall between the sacred and secular, declaring that in kingdom terms everything is sacred. The dividing line is not between sacred and secular but between the kingdom of God and the kingdom of darkness.

We still suffer under the false notion that the religious realm lies in the sacred, private sphere. The sacred is associated with the church, the family and the interior commitments of individuals. Religion is a private affair that has little influence on the public arenas of life—the workplace, politics and other major institutions of society such as economics, education and the media. A newly converted vice president at NBC was asked how his new faith would affect the moral standards of programming at NBC. Buying in to the sacred-secular bifurcation, he said, "All it does is give me peace of mind in my personal life. But whether it will affect my programming, it doesn't. It just makes me think clearer, but that just means I will probably think more commercially than I did before."[15]

There is a disconnect for many Christians when it comes to seeing ourselves as representatives of the kingdom of God in what we spend most of our time doing—our jobs. Many fellow believers unconsciously take off their Christian hat and put on their secular hat when they walk through the doorway of the workplace. It is assumed that we play by a different set of rules when it comes to our secular employment versus the way we live in the sacred realm. How out of step this is with Jesus' message of the kingdom!

Rate your ministry on a scale of 1 to 5, with 1 being private faith and 5 being holistic discipleship.		
DISCIPLESHIP SYMPTOM	RATING	NOTES
Private faith . . . Holistic discipleship		

4. A countercultural force. The Scriptures picture the Christian community as a countercultural force; the reality is that we see isolated individuals whose lifestyle and values are not much different from those of the unchurched.

Stott describes the church of the Lord's intention as a community of "radical non-conformity." This phrase is a helpful summary of some of the biblical metaphors for the church. The images of alien, exile and sojourner capture the relationship of believers to this present world (1 Peter 2:11). This sentiment is expressed in the words of the old hymn, "This world is not my home, I'm just a-passin' through." The church in the biblical scheme is a body whose collective lifestyle forms a countercultural alternative to the values of the dominant society.

The apostle Peter gave us a word picture for this new reality when he addressed the church dispersed across the landscape of the Greco-Roman world. Though these believers in Jesus did not have a land to call their own, he could still say to them, "You are . . . a holy nation" (1 Peter 2:9). By using this image Peter was saying, "You are a people who cut across all geopolitical boundaries, because you are a church without borders." To be holy is to be a called-out people, meaning separate or different. One of the key distinguishing features of this new kingdom people is their lifestyle of compassionate and costly service. Echoing Jesus' words in the Sermon on the Mount (Matthew 5:16), Peter says, "Conduct yourselves honorably among the Gentiles, so that, though they malign you as evildoers, they may see your honorable deeds and glorify God when he comes to judge" (1 Peter 2:12). Those hostile to the church may not affirm what you believe, but they can't argue against the way you live.

If that was true then, what is it that people see today when they look at the church? Many observers have concluded that the church, far from being countercultural, does not look much different from the unchurched. After looking at a number of categories of lifestyle and values, Barna concluded, "The fact that the proportion of Christians who affirm these values is equivalent to the proportion of non-Christians who hold similar views indicates how meaningless Christianity has been in the lives of millions of professed believers."[16] Regarding materialism and measuring success, half the Christian public never has enough money to buy what they need or want. One in four Christians thinks the more you have, the more successful you are.

The church is not immune to the diseases of individualism and consumerism dominant in American society. Sociologist Robert Bellah searched for the core characteristic that defines the American character. In his landmark study *Habits of the Heart* Bellah says that what makes Americans distinct comes down to one thing, a view of freedom. Yet when we look more closely, we see a one-sided view of freedom. Americans want freedom *from* rather than freedom *for,* an attitude of "I want to do what I want to do when I want to do it. No one better tell me otherwise." Bellah concludes that this quality is not the stuff on which to build enduring relationships (such as marriage) or deep community. To the extent that the church is reduced to an aggregate of individuals who shop like consumers to meet their needs, we do not have the basis for community in any biblical sense. How can we possibly build countercultural communities out of such porous material?

Rate your ministry on a scale of 1 to 5, with 1 being blending in and 5 being countercultural force.		
DISCIPLESHIP SYMPTOM	RATING	NOTES
Blending in . . . Countercultural force		

5. An essential, chosen organism. The Scriptures picture the church as an essential, chosen organism in whom Christ dwells; the reality is that people view the church as an optional institution, unnecessary for discipleship.

The church of Jesus Christ is nothing less than his corporate replacement on earth. Jesus continues his incarnation by dwelling in his people. The late Ray Stedman succinctly described Christ's relationship to the church: "The life of Jesus is still being manifest among people, but now no longer through an individual physical body, limited to one place on earth, but through a complex, corporate body called the church."[17] The apostle Paul's favorite and most fundamental image for the church is that of the body of Christ. When Paul uses this phrase, it is far more than a nice word picture or metaphor. He is not saying that the church is *like* the body of Christ but that it literally *is* the body of Christ. This is the place where Christ dwells.

The implication that follows is that the church is not an optional afterthought for those who name Christ as their Lord. The church is central to God's plan of salvation. God saves people into a new community, which is the vanguard of a new humanity. To be called to Christ is to throw in one's lot with his people. Many people today like to say, "Jesus, yes; church, no." To do so is a fundamental misunderstanding of the place that the church has in God's grand scheme of salvation. To be a follower of Christ is to understand that there is no such thing as solo discipleship.

Yet this optional attitude toward the church surfaces in our individualistic, take-our-own-counsel culture. How does this optional attitude express itself?

One such expression is that being integrally involved in the church is not a necessity for Christian living. My wife and I visited a well-known Southern California church the Sunday following Easter. The message was directed toward the twenty-one hundred people who had indicated they made a decision to receive Christ during the Easter services. The teacher of the morning asked the worshipers, "Is it necessary to go to church or be a part of the church to be a Christian?" His answer? "No, it is not necessary." I had to do everything I could not to bolt from my seat and shout, "Yes, it is absolutely necessary to be a part of the church if you are a Christian!" But that is not the prevailing wisdom, apparently even from those who should know better.

Christian leaders live with the tension of serving a community of people with a tenuous commitment. How do you call people to the discipline of discipleship when they can easily walk on you? Unless there is a covenantal understanding of a believer's relationship with a community, how can people be formed into Christlike disciples?

Rate your ministry on a scale of 1 to 5, with 1 being church is optional and 5 being church is essential.		
DISCIPLESHIP SYMPTOM	RATING	NOTES
Church is optional . . . Church is essential		

6. Biblically informed people. The Scriptures picture believers as biblically informed people whose lives are founded on revealed truth; the reality is that most believers are biblically ignorant people whose lives are a syncretistic compromise.

The Scripture of the Old and New Testaments is the trustworthy depository of God's self-revelation to humanity. This is the historic Christian confession about the uniqueness of the Bible. Jesus Christ is the Word made flesh, while the Bible is the God-breathed written Word that is the reliable witness to his actions in history. Although truth can be found beyond Scripture, the test of what is true is anchored in the written Word of God. This belief about the book we call the Bible has made it the source of our public teaching, the object of disciplined devotional reading and the truth around which small groups gather. The twin disciplines of prayer and Bible reading have been promoted as the activities that should dominate a believer's daily devotional practice.

Yet in spite of what we affirm about the uniqueness of this book, Christians in general are ignorant of its content and hold convictions that are contrary to its clear and central teaching. About the disjunction between the attitude that people have about the Bible and their knowledge of it, Gallup has written, "Americans revere the Bible—but, by and large, they don't read it."[18] According to Gallup, 65 percent of the adult population agree that the Bible "answers all or most of the basic questions of life."[19] Barna's surveys found that 60 percent of all American adults and 85 percent who described themselves as born again would affirm the statement "The Bible is totally accurate in all that it teaches." In spite of these affirmations there is an appalling ignorance of the book we put on a pedestal. For example, 53 percent of the adults in Barna's survey believed that the saying "God helps those who help themselves" is a biblical truth.

But even more disturbing than not knowing certain factual data is holding basic beliefs that are contrary to biblical affirmation. Of all Americans, 61 percent believed that the Holy Spirit is not a living entity but a symbol of God's presence and power, whereas 58 percent believed the devil or Satan is not a living being but only a symbol of evil. Perhaps the most disturbing finding was that four out ten people actively involved in Christian discipleship relationships believed that there is no such thing as absolute truth.[20]

Only a generation ago, two Christian prophets, Francis Schaeffer and Elton Trueblood, predicted that we were one generation away from losing the memory of Christianity in our culture. They both referred to America as a "cut-flower" society. By that they meant that our culture has been severed from its Judeo-Christian roots and that we are living on the memory of faith. They predicted that it would take just one more generation for this memory to fade. We are that generation. Preachers and teachers of the Word can no longer assume that mention of the biblical figures like David and Goliath will instantly draw the story to people's memories. No assumptions can be made about what people know or the beliefs they hold.

Rate your ministry on a scale of 1 to 5, with 1 being biblically illiterate and 5 being biblically informed.		
DISCIPLESHIP SYMPTOM	RATING	NOTES
Biblically illiterate . . . Biblically informed		

7. *People who share their faith.* The Scriptures picture all believers as those who share the story of their faith in Christ with others; the reality is we are an intimidated people who shrink from personal witness.

We are storytellers. The Bible spins a love story of God's pursuit of wayward humanity. Those who have been captured by Jesus Christ have a story to tell of how God chased us down and embraced us in his loving arms. In so doing, the Lord has written us as characters into his grand redemptive drama. We each have an assigned part to play on the stage of history, which is the realm in which God writes his story. It is this story that makes sense of why we are here. As unique as each of us is, there is a common story line written into the script for each of our lives. "You will be my witnesses," Jesus says (Acts 1:8). We each have our story and *the* story to tell, for in the sharing of our story and *the* story, others come to find that they too have been written into this redemptive drama. Paul could not be clearer about the privilege that is ours when he wrote that the gospel "is the power of God for salvation" (Romans 1:16). God has entrusted to us the story of the visited planet, and telling it is the means that he uses to melt human hearts.

How are we doing in telling the story? On the surface the picture appears to be quite positive, but it gets cloudier upon closer examination. Of those who identified themselves as born again, 55 percent said that they had shared their faith in Christ with someone in the last year with the hope of seeing that person become a follower of Christ.[21] Yet when they were asked if they have intentionally built a relationship with someone with the hope of being able to lead the person to Christ, only one in ten could affirm that they had. "Fewer than one in five said that they knew a non-believer well enough that they could share their faith with an individual in a context of trust and credibility."[22] Another way this need has been dramatized is that it takes 100 members of a congregation to win 1.67 people to Christ in a given year. This indicates that a small percentage of people are active in a personal witness to the gospel.

In my experience as a pastor, it appears that a small percentage of a congregation have the confidence and motivation to share their gospel story with others. A major contributor to this inhibition is the intimidation that comes from living in a culture that shuns absolute truth. The only truth that is recognized is personal truth. Each person has his or her individual truth, while no one else's truth should be imposed upon another. This has the effect of putting all truth claims on an equal plane. Since the god of this age is maximum choice, any belief that lays claim to be *the* truth will be met with indignation. On many occasions I have braced myself for the pushback, "You mean to tell me if I don't accept Christ I am going to hell?" Each time I swallowed hard and somewhat reluctantly said, "Jesus is the one in whom God has revealed himself and through him made provision for us to be made right with him." It seems so intolerant in an age where tolerance is equated with grace.

In this atmosphere of intimidation, we must ask ourselves what we have to offer. Do we truly believe that we have something that is so vital and personally life giving that we have something to give away? Another way to look at this might be, do we want someone else to have the same fulfilling relationship with God that we do? Bill Hybels, senior pastor at Willow Creek Community Church, says that seekers look at our lives and ask themselves, "If I become a Christian, am I trading up or trading down?"[23] So the question becomes, is our experience of the love and joy of Jesus worth transmitting to others? For many, it is not.

Rate your ministry on a scale of 1 to 5, with 1 being shrinking from personal witness and 5 being sharing our faith.		
DISCIPLESHIP SYMPTOM	RATING	NOTES
Shrinking from personal witness . . . Sharing our faith		

THE IMPOSSIBLE POSSIBILITY: WHERE ARE WE GOING?

Is this an accurate picture of the state of discipleship today? Overly dire? Does this picture accord with your reality? If this portrait of the gap between the biblical standard and the current state of discipleship is close to being accurate, then there is enormous work to be done if the gap is to be closed.

What is our intended destination? Joel Barker helps us to focus our goal with what he calls the paradigm shift question: "What is impossible to do in your business [read church or ministry], but if it could be done, would fundamentally change it?"[24] The following is my vote for the paradigm shift question that expresses the impossible possibility: How can we grow self-initiating, reproducing, fully devoted followers of Jesus Christ?

This strategic question is a way of asking how we might fulfill what Jesus said is the mission of his church. Jesus saved every church considerable time and effort when he wrote the mission statement that gives us our marching orders: "Go therefore and make disciples [of me] of all nations" (Matthew 28:19). What is a disciple of Jesus but one who is self-initiating, reproducing and fully devoted to him? What seems unattainable is that there would be churches filled with disciples who do not have to be pushed, motivated and cajoled.

My goal in this chapter has been to bring into stark focus the impossible possibility. It is to this impossible possibility that leaders must speak. John Kotter in *Leading Change* says that the primary reason why change does not occur is that there is no sense of urgency.[25] Leadership is about instilling urgency, which comes about by defining reality and calling God's people to the possibilities and dreams of what God intended us to be.

Only as we soberly assess the way things are can we have any hope of getting to the way things were designed to be. We have hope because Jesus as the Lord of the church seeks for his bride to be without spot and blemish, for through his church his life will be manifest. Barna has written, "Christianity would be incredibly influential in our culture if Christians consistently lived their faith. Most non-Christians don't read the Bible, so they judge Christianity by the lives of the Christians they see. The problem is that millions of Christians don't live like Christians—and that's partially because they don't know what they believe and therefore cannot apply appropriate scriptural values to their lives."[26]

How have we gotten to this state of discipleship? It is one thing to describe where we are. It is another to identify the root causes of the problem. In the next chapter, we will complete our portrait of reality by identifying the contributing factors that have diverted us from making self-initiating, reproducing, fully devoted followers of Jesus as the central mission of the church. When we know and face the causes of our low level of discipleship, then we can begin to address them.

2

THE DISCIPLESHIP MALAISE
Getting to the Root Causes

What chances of survival would you give an organization in which 20 percent of its members do the work while 80 percent pick and choose their level of participation? Only about one-sixth of the members make regular efforts to understand the mission of the organization and their part in carrying it out. Though the members declare the organization's training manual to be their guiding vision, the majority spend little time reading it in order to live by it. When the members are involved in their public roles outside the organization, most people with whom they associate would not have any idea that this organization has meaning in their life. So blended have the members become with the rest of the world that they appear to be indistinguishable from those who have no association with this organization. In fact, the majority of participants in the organization view their membership as optional, not a necessity for living by the organization's ideals.

If the church were simply of human origin, we might not be hopeful that this organization had any future. Since the church is God's plan for redemption of the world, we have absolute confidence that our Lord will restore it to the purpose for which he designed it—to make disciples of all nations. He said that his followers would be the light of the world and the salt of the earth.

In this chapter I will address the causes for discipleship malaise. If we were to take today's church to a clinic for a health checkup, how would the church doctor diagnose the symptoms? The diagnosis might include eight factors that have contributed to the church's failure to grow self-initiating, reproducing, fully devoted followers of Jesus.

DIVERSION FROM PRIMARY CALLING

The first cause of the low estate of discipleship is that pastors have been diverted from their primary calling to "equip the saints for the work of ministry."

The New Testament does not give us an extended job description for the role that pastors and elders are to play vis-à-vis the whole people of God, but what we are given is clear. The nearest thing to a pastoral job description is found in the oft-quoted Ephesians 4:12, which says that those given to the church as its leaders are "to equip the saints for the work of ministry." In my book *Unfinished Business*[1] there is an extended exploration of the meaning of the term *equip*.[2] Leaders in the church have been assigned the task of preparing or training ordinary believers, referred to as saints, for their place of service in the body of Christ. The whole people of God are the ministers, while the church staff are the administers.[3] In other words, leaders exist to serve the servants and therefore to provide the encouragement and training so the ministers can minister. If the pastor-teachers and other leaders fulfill their biblically prescribed role, then positive consequences naturally follow: the body of Christ is built up, a unity of faith is grounded in the knowledge of God's Son, and the church grows to maturity, "fully developed within and without, fully alive like Christ" (Ephesians 4:12-13 The Message).

If I were Satan and wanted to fatally stunt the growth of disciples to maturity, what would I do? I would divert the leaders from fulfilling their God-given function of equipping the saints. Instead, I would distract them with other good and high-sounding activities that have nothing to do with growing people to maturity and engaging them in ministry. This is exactly what has happened. We have shunted our spiritual leaders into being program developers, administrators and caregivers.

One role, pastoral care, has consumed pastors. Assigning caregiving to the professionals has had a disastrous impact on people's ability to grow up to adulthood in the faith. Pastors are fully aware that a major portion of their job is to respond to the care needs of their members and constituents. If someone is in the hospital or grieving the death of a loved one or experiencing a life-altering setback such as a loss of a job, marital difficulties or a rebellious child, the pastor is expected to be present. The emotional contract between people and pastor in most of our churches is "If I am having difficulty, Pastor, I expect you to be there to get me through it. If you don't show up, you are failing to do the job that pastors are supposed to do. If you have failed in providing care, you have failed as a pastor."

Assigning care to professionals has turned pastors into responders. I was leading a two-day seminar for Methodist pastors in a southern state. To a person, the pastors came tethered to their beepers and cell phones. Their pastoral ministry centered on dropping everything when their parishioners claimed to need them at their side. What makes pastoral care so alluring is that it appears to be so high-minded. What better way to exemplify the servant ministry of Jesus than respond to another's call? But how does caring for those in need "equip the saints for works of service"?

The good is always the enemy of the best. The apostles faced this temptation during the early stages of church life. A dispute arose in the church in Jerusalem because the Greek-speaking widows thought they were being slighted in the daily distribution of the food. This problem was laid at the apostles' feet. Here was an opportunity for the apostles to act as true servants and model care to the whole church. But the apostles decided that serving tables was not their primary call. They rightly saw this ministry opportunity as a diversion from their call to preach the word and to pray. "It is not right that we should neglect the word of God in order to wait on tables" (Acts 6:2). They refused to do so, not because it was beneath their dignity but because it was not their God-assigned call. To the extent that they refused to take on what was not theirs, they expanded ministry opportunities for others.

To the extent that pastors have taken on what is not theirs, they accept a task that has been assigned to the church—to care for one another. While pastoral care is sometimes needed, for the most part the church members should minister to one another. Pastors are busy with caregiving duties instead of investing in leadership development, discipling individuals to maturity, teaching people how to discern their call to ministry, managing a ministry culture where people are ministering to one another or visiting parishioners in the workplace. The saints' ability to minister remains woefully underdeveloped, since pastors do focus on growing people to maturity and deploying them in ministry.

We have an undiscipled church because its leaders have not made discipling their primary focus.

DISCIPLING THROUGH PROGRAMS

The second cause of the low estate of discipleship is that we have tried to make disciples through programs.

The scriptural context for growing disciples is through relationships. Jesus called the Twelve to be with him, for through personal association their lives would be transformed. Proximity produces disciples. The apostle Paul had his Timothies who were ministry partners, for in this side-by-side ministry, leaders could be trained to carry on after his departure. Disciples are made in "iron sharpens iron" intentional relationships.

In today's church we have replaced person-centered growth with programs as the means of making disciples. By programs I mean the structured group methods we use to herd large groups of people through systems. Examples of programs are age-graded Sunday schools, adult education classes, small-group ministries, need-based seminars or highly structured discipleship programs.

All of these programs can contribute to discipleship development, but they miss the central ingredient in discipleship. Each disciple is a unique individual who grows at a rate peculiar to him or her. Unless disciples receive personal attention so that their particular growth needs are addressed in a way that calls them to die to self and live fully to Christ, a disciple will not be made.

Since individual, personal investment is costly and time-intensive, we have put programs in its place. As George Barna says, programs "are often embraced as a way of organizing large groups of people into an orderly process that can be easily managed and controlled. If we were to be honest, we would have to admit that the absence of real measures of personal growth are a testimony to our concern about style more than substance, and our commitment to taking action more than having impact."[4] In other words, programs can make it look like we are growing disciples, but that is more illusion than reality, and we know it.

Why don't programs make disciples? As I see it, programs have four characteristics in common.

Programs tend to be information- or knowledge-based. Programs operate on the assumption that if someone has information, having that information will automatically lead to transformation. In other words, right knowledge will produce right living. We can find the flaw in this reasoning, however, from the example of Elvis Presley. As a child, he went to a church camp for five consecutive summers for free by memorizing 350 verses of Scripture each year. That means that 1,750 Bible passages were tucked away in the recesses of his memory. Yet the content of these verses alone was not sufficient to keep Elvis Presley focused on a lifestyle pleasing to God.

As one who has been a pastor and a professor, I do not oppose acquiring knowledge. But information alone does not lead to transformation. We can hold truth in a compartmentalized fashion without having it change the way we think, feel or act. James made the same observation when he said that faith apart from works is dead. We can subscribe to a set of beliefs without allowing them to affect our lifestyle. To drive home his point James writes, "Even the demons believe [in God]—and shudder" (James 2:19). We have tended to view the teaching process as the teacher with the full pitcher emptying its contents into the student's empty pitcher. It is simply a process of information transfer. Since Christlikeness is our goal, we must ask, how does more information by itself accomplish that?

Programs are the one preparing for the many. Most programs are built around an individual or a few core people who do the hard work of preparation. The rest come, to a greater or lesser degree, as passive recipients of their work. Though this may provide tremendous benefit to ones who have done the preparation, the result is usually enormous amounts of unprocessed information. The classic example of this is preaching. As much as I believe in the power of preaching for conviction and decision, I would be naive to believe that preaching alone produces disciples. If preaching could produce disciples, the job of making disciples would be done.

During my season as a seminary professor, I had the opportunity to sit in the congregation as a worshiper. This allowed time to reflect on what happens or does not happen in this setting. I have concluded that the preached word needs the context of community, where meaning can be discussed and bold implications for our lives heard. When the worship service is over, much of what happened in worship is lost by the time people move to the patio to engage in their first conversation.

Programs are characterized by regimentation or synchronization. The nature of most programs is that they do not take into account an individual's growth rate, which is essential to growing disciples. When more than four people gather, one must set up a system in which people are required to move through content in a coordinated fashion. So we have programs that are ten weeks (or thirty weeks, or whatever the length of time) to making disciples. The idea is that people cover identical content in the same sequence at the same rate. Completing the program is equated with making disciples.

What this conjures up in my mind is the modern approach to mass production. We attempt to make disciples in the same way we construct a car. When the process is completed, disciples are supposed to pop out the other end of the production line. But regimentation and synchronization are counterproductive in disciple making. Every individual is unique and different. Making disciples requires a customized approach. This means that a person's knowledge; character growth; obedience in thought, word and deed; discernment of unique ministry identity; and so on all need to be dealt with in the context of Jesus' radical and total claim upon an individual's life in the setting of community. Barna concludes, "Few churches intentionally guide their people through a strategic learning and developmental process that has been customized for the student."[5]

Programs generally have low personal accountability. How many of us have anyone to hold us accountable to our obedience to Jesus Christ? Programs of discipleship often give the illusion of accountability. But on closer examination the focus is on completing the assigned study curriculum rather than committing to life change. Barna puts it like this: "Few churches have systems by which they measure what is happening in the life of church adherents. Few believers have lined up a trustworthy and competent partner who will hold them accountable to specific and measurable goals."[6]

Though all approaches to disciple making will have programmatic elements, such as structure and curriculum (even if it is the Bible), the growth process of the individual is always preeminent in a relational setting.

REDUCING THE CHRISTIAN LIFE

The third cause of the low estate of discipleship is that we have reduced the Christian life to the eternal benefits we get from Jesus, rather than living as students of Jesus.

Jesus clearly defined his intention for the church's mission in what we call the Great Commission and what others have cynically referred to as the Great Omission. Jesus gave the mission statement for all churches when he said, "Go therefore and make disciples of all nations" (Mathew 28:19). He didn't stop there and make us guess as to when a disciple was made. Jesus said that disciples are to be baptized into the name of the Father, Son and Holy Spirit (identity submerged into the triune God) and to be taught to observe or obey all that he commanded. In other words, a disciple is one who, in the context of community, places himself or herself under the shaping influence of Jesus so that there is no doubt as to who is deploying the formative power.

Dallas Willard, a prophetic voice, has pointed out how far we have strayed from understanding the Christian life as sitting at the feet of Jesus. Instead we focus on the benefits that we receive by faith in Jesus rather than on being conformed to the life of Jesus. We want abundance without obedience. Willard calls this "bar-code" Christianity. We are merely concerned with being read by the great scanner in the sky as possessing eternal life. What is it that allows the scanner to read our bar code? Playing off the bumper sticker "Christians aren't perfect, just forgiven," Willard sees in this phrase how we have reduced the Christian life to receiving forgiveness. When is a Christian a Christian? Depending upon our tradition, it is when we embrace the gift of eternal life (forgiveness) by saying the sinner's prayer, walking the aisle to the kneeling rail, inviting Jesus quietly into our heart or receiving the sacrament of baptism. The bottom line essential within the evangelical world is having the debt of one's sins canceled by transferring them to Jesus' account.

Willard challenges us to look at the product and ask how we got here. "Should we not at least consider the possibility that this poor result is not in spite of what we teach and how we teach, but precisely because of it?"[7] Reducing the Christian life to embracing the gift of forgiveness has made obedience to Jesus in daily life an irrelevance. Willard writes, "The most telling thing about the contemporary Christian is that he or she simply has no compelling sense that understanding of and conformity with the clear teachings of Christ is of any vital importance to his or her life, and certainly not that it is in any way essential."[8] How else do we account for the disjunction between professed faith and the quality of discipleship? There must be something fundamentally wrong with the way we have been teaching what it means to be a Christian.

What is that? We have not called people into an apprentice relationship with Jesus. Jesus is not looked to as our discipler, teacher and Lord. We do not see him as the compelling figure who is our trainer in this life. "The fact is that there now is lacking a serious and expectant intention to bring Jesus' people into obedience and abundance through training. That would be discipleship as he gave it to us."[9] If we did believe this, we might see more classes in the church with titles like "How to Genuinely Bless Someone Who Is Spitting on You" or "How to Live Without Indulging in Lust or Covetousness." It is our lack of intention to conform to Christ's teaching that makes class titles like these sound startling.

Willard is right when he says we have disconnected the Christian life from the person who called us to follow him. Instead we have taken the benefits of forgiveness with a positively altered state of inner peace and equated the Christian life with being a decent person.

A Two-Tiered Understanding of Discipleship

The fourth cause of the low estate of discipleship is that we have made discipleship for super-Christians, not ordinary believers.

There appears to be a two-tiered understanding of what it means to be a Christian. Michael Wilkins, professor of New Testament and dean of the faculty at Talbot Seminary, regularly asks two questions when he speaks to groups about discipleship. The contrasting answers to these questions give us insight into the way that people understand discipleship. The first question is, "How many of you can say, in the humble confidence of your heart, that you are true disciples of Jesus? Please raise your hand." Wilkins says that people are genuinely confused as to what they should do. Most do not raise their hand. Some put it up hesitantly and then quickly pull it down. Then Wilkins proceeds to a second question: "How many of you can say, in the humble confidence of your heart, that you are convinced that you are a true Christian? Please raise your hand." Immediately most hands go up without hesitation.[10]

Why is it that people can affirm being true Christians but are hesitant about identifying themselves as true disciples of Jesus? My guess is that for those who see themselves as true Christians it has nothing to do with the quality of their Christianity. True Christians are those ones who have received the gift of salvation and are viewed by Christ through the eyes of grace. So being true Christians is not something of their own doing but something done for them, whereas being true disciples of Jesus is a statement of personal evaluation as to how consistent or committed they are in following the one they claim to be Lord.

When Jesus says, "If any want to become my followers, let them deny themselves and take up their cross daily and follow me" (Luke 9:23), is he intending this to be the standard for all who name him as Savior? The empirical answer to that is apparently no. Many people have clearly made a distinction between being a

Christian and being a disciple. For some, the difference is the level of commitment. Dwight Pentecost writes, "There is a vast difference between being a Christian and being a disciple."[11] The difference is commitment. There are ordinary believers who have slipped into the kingdom through profession of faith in Christ, and then there are those who have died to self in response to Jesus' call. Others would make a similar two-tiered distinction but base it on the call to a profession. There are ordinary believers and then there is a set-apart class of people we refer to as pastors, missionaries, and so on.

A close examination of biblical discipleship does not allow for two classes of followers: the ordinary and extraordinary. There are Christians who have not lived up to the expectations of a disciple yet can still be called Christians, but that in no way lets them off the hook. Paul refers to Christians who have not progressed as babes in Christ who are still drinking milk, when they should be taking solid food (1 Corinthians 3:1-3). Paul's scolding believers for not growing to maturity, as they should, is a long way from building into our theology that there are first-class and second-class disciples.

We need to recapture the biblical expectation defined by Jesus when he said, "If *any* want to become my followers" (Luke 9:23). This was Jesus' starting point.

UNWILLINGNESS TO CALL PEOPLE TO DISCIPLESHIP

The fifth cause of the low estate of discipleship is that leaders have been unwilling to call people to discipleship.

Christian leaders seem to be reluctant to restate the terms of discipleship that Jesus laid out. What are the reasons for our reluctance? We are afraid that if we ask too much, people will stop coming to our churches. Our operating assumption is that people will flee to the nearby entertainment church if we ask them to give too much of themselves. So we start with a low bar and try to entice people by increments of commitment, hoping that we can raise the bar imperceptibly to the ultimate destination of discipleship. In our post-Christian world, the common wisdom is to lure seekers to our message by helping them see the faith's relevance to life's daily challenges. This usually means appealing to self-interest, felt need, personal fulfillment or a person's search for happiness. Oftentimes the message received is that it is all about me, not about finding me only as I lose myself into Jesus.

If we start with a no-pain gospel, then it will only become disillusioning, for it will not deliver what was promised. I know how empty the no-pain promises can be. I believe the infomercials for exercise equipment that tell me that I can lose weight and have rock-hard abs in only three minutes a day. My wife and daughter ridicule me mercilessly for having accumulated the worthless gadgets in my exercise equipment graveyard. Just as the no-pain promises in the fitness field leave me feeling foolish, the same is true with our terms of discipleship. Jesus pleases only when we come to him on his terms. It is when we lose our life for his sake that we find it.

Finally, the unwillingness of leaders to call people to commitment may reveal something frighteningly personal. Perhaps our unwillingness to put Jesus' term on the line is rooted in our reluctance to live a no-holds-barred commitment ourselves. Are we willing to live the message we want to put before the people we serve? Since discipleship is more caught than taught, as much model as message, it calls us to a level of self-examination that can be uncomfortable. Could it be that our unwillingness to set the bar high for our congregations is because we want to let ourselves off the hook? If we call people to a higher level, are we ourselves willing to enter that adventure? To paraphrase Willard, is the quality of discipleship we are getting not in spite of our leadership but because of it?

The irony is that the fear of losing people if we call them to commitment is unfounded. Growing churches generally have appealed to idealism and sacrifice by calling people to join the greatest enterprise launched on this planet—God's rescue mission through his church.

AN INADEQUATE VIEW OF THE CHURCH

The sixth cause of the low estate of discipleship is that we have an inadequate view of the church as a discipleship community.

In chapter one I mentioned that many view the church as an option, not a requirement, when it comes to living the Christian life. In order to view the church in this way, one must have an inadequate understanding of the place of the church in God's redemptive plan. Biblically, discipleship is never seen as a me-and-Jesus solo relationship, for the church is a discipleship community.

This is Paul's message to the church at Corinth: "You are the body of Christ [corporately] and individually members of it" (1 Corinthians 12:27). Not only is God saving individuals, but he also is forming a people. Our identity as believers is found and shaped in community. Paul strikes a perfect balance between our relationship to the community and our identity as individuals. In the church our individuality is maintained. We are not drops of water consumed by the ocean. Yet at the same time we don't have an individual identity apart from the church. Our value as believers is known by playing our God-assigned part in building up the church through the avenue of our spiritual gifts. The Christian life is inherently communal.

We live at a time of radical individualism that has torn the heart out of Christian community. Robert Putnam, in *Bowling Alone: The Collapse and Revival of American Community,* makes the convincing case that the social capital of religious life is being undermined by privatized faith. The collective strength of the church has been weakened by the trend over the last generation toward isolated, personalized belief. Putnam quotes Wade Clark Roof and William McKinney:

Large numbers of young, well-educated, middle-class youth . . . defected from the churches in the late sixties and the seventies. . . . Some joined new religious movements, others sought personal enlightenment through various spiritual therapies and disciplines, but most simply "dropped out" of organized religion altogether. . . . [The consequence was a] tendency toward highly individualized religious psychology without the benefits of strong supportive attachments to believing communities. A major impetus in this direction in the post-1960's was the thrust toward greater personal fulfillment and quest for the ideal self. . . . In this climate of expressive individualism, religion tends to become "privatized" and more anchored in the personal realms.[12]

The church has allowed this trend toward privatized faith to undermine the tight-knit community that is needed if disciples are to be formed. Jesus said that our love for one another (John 13:34-35) and our visible unity (John 17:20-23) would be signs that we are his disciples and that he was sent from the Father. These qualities need to be at the heart of a disciple-making community. Yet our lack of commitment to covenantal community makes this ultimate apologetic only a wistful hope. As a member of Rotary International, if I missed four meetings in a row I was automatically dropped from membership. I would dare say that the mission of the church of Jesus Christ outstrips the mission of Rotary, yet we tend not to set comparable expectations. Given our weak understanding of the church as community, how can we possibly act as servants to another or care enough to be unified with other believers?

No Clear Pathway to Maturity

The seventh cause of the low estate of discipleship is that most churches have no clear, public pathway to maturity.

If making disciples is the primary mission of the church, would we not expect some public pathway to maturity in Christ in most churches? Yet it is rare to find a church with a well-thought-out, easy-to-grasp process or path onto which people can get if they want to become self-initiating, reproducing, fully devoted followers of Christ. We have no destination in mind, and so therefore no road on which people can walk even if they want to understand the implications of discipleship.

Rick Warren, pastor of Saddleback Community Church in Southern California, has developed the most popular and copied public discipleship model, which he calls the Life Development Process. This process is pictured in the recognizable form of a baseball diamond. Adaptations of this scheme can be found in many a church. First base is the covenant of membership, by which one makes a commitment to Jesus Christ. Second base is the covenant of maturity, by which a person commits to basic spiritual disciplines for growth. Third base is the covenant of ministry, by which one discovers and commits to be involved in ministry consistent with one's spiritual gifts, heart, abilities, personality and life experience (SHAPE). Home plate expresses commitment to missions, touching felt need through compassionate service and offering a witness to Jesus Christ with the hope of bringing others into a saving relationship. The pitcher's mound at the center of the baseball diamond conveys that everything centers on the fifth purpose of the church, which is magnification or worship.

Though this model has been criticized as simplistic and not recognizing the shaping influence of life's setbacks, the genius of this model is that it is a quickly graspable, progressive image of what it means to move more deeply into the life of following Jesus Christ. Warren states, "Instead of growing a church with programs, focus on growing people with a process. We need a process to go with purpose. Unless the purpose is fleshed out in a process, then we don't have anything but nice platitudes."[13] The church, says Warren, needs to clearly define its purposes and then organize around them so that there is a sequential process to accomplish them in the lives of believers.

This clarity of purpose and connection to process are missing in most churches. Barna's research concluded, "Relatively small numbers of born again adults said that their churches gives them the specific paths to follow to foster growth. Slightly less than half said their churches had identified any spiritual goals, standards or expectations for the congregation in the past year. . . . Only one out of every five believers stated that their church has some means of facilitating an evaluation of the spiritual maturity or commitment to maturity of their congregation."[14] However, nine out of ten believers in this same survey said they would take seriously their church's recommendation to pursue a spiritual path if one was presented to them.

LACK OF PERSONAL DISCIPLING

The eighth and final cause of the low estate of discipleship is that most Christians have never been personally discipled.

I now come to the burden that is at the heart of this book. This takes us back to our paradigm shift question: How can we grow Christians into self-initiating, reproducing, fully devoted followers of Jesus Christ? My conviction is that the primary way people grow into self-initiating, reproducing, fully devoted followers of Jesus Christ is by being involved in highly accountable, relational, multiplying discipleship units of three or four.

A major reason for the seven previously identified flaws in the life of the Christian church is that people have not been personally discipled. By discipling I mean "a process that takes place within accountable relationships over a period of time for the purpose of bringing believers to spiritual maturity in Christ."[15] Over the last seventeen years that I have been conducting workshops on discipleship, I have asked thousands of believers, "How many of you have been in an intentional discipleship relationship in which someone has walked with you over time with the express purpose of helping you become mature in Christ?" Approximately 10 to 15 percent of the people raise their hands. This is probably an unusually high percentage in comparison with the ordinary church population. After all, those at a seminar on discipling have already demonstrated that they are a part of the 20 percent involved in the church community.

It is my contention that a necessary and pivotal element in providing the motivation and discipline to grow self-initiating, reproducing, fully devoted followers of Jesus comes only through personal investment. The motivation and discipline will not ultimately occur through listening to sermons, sitting in a class, participating in a fellowship group, attending a study group in the workplace or being a member of a small group, but rather in the context of highly accountable, relationally transparent, truth-centered, small (three or four people) discipleship units. In my experience this is the optimum context for transformation. If every believer had this opportunity, we would go a long way toward addressing the causes of the discipleship malaise I have sketched throughout this chapter. Barna comments on this as well: "A majority (55%) of the adults who indicated their interest in hearing advice on how to improve their spiritual life also said that if the church matched them with a spiritual mentor or coach, they would be more likely to pursue the changes suggested to them."[16]

When the product we are producing in our churches has so departed from what Jesus said we are to make, we must stop and ask, *Where have we gone wrong?* If the picture I have painted is close to reality, it should cause us to shudder and weep. We must plead to the One who gave us our marching orders and ask, "Lord, how can we get back on track to making quality disciples, which you said is our mission?"

Before going on, take a few minutes to do your reality assessment. Examine each of the causes of discipleship deficit in light of your ministry. To each give a numerical rating between 1 and 5, with 1 being completely true and 5 being not true at all.

CAUSES OF DISCIPLESHIP DEFICIT	RATING	NOTES
Diversion from primary calling		
Discipling through programs		
Reducing the Christian life		
A two-tiered understanding of discipleship		
Unwillingness to call people to discipleship		
An inadequate view of the church		
No clear pathway to maturity		
Lack of personal discipling		

The next chapters of this book take us into a review of the biblical vision of how disciples are made. In these chapters we will examine the models of our Lord Jesus and the apostle Paul. We have lost sight of the obvious. Jesus showed how we are to develop people by his selection of the Twelve and his investment in their lives over a three-year period. Paul's life ambition was to "present everyone mature," also through personal investment. George Orwell wrote a generation ago, "We have now sunk to a depth at which the re-statement of the obvious is the first duty of intelligent men."[17] My hope is that by walking with Jesus and Paul in their school of disciple making, we will own the imperative that we too must do the Lord's work in the Lord's way.

PART TWO

Doing the Lord's Work in the Lord's Way

The Bible as a Method Book

3

Why Jesus Invested in a Few

I remember the phone call quite well. What I didn't know at the time was how much it would change my life. Don was on the other end of the line. He was a seminary student working as an intern at my church during my college years. Don had begun an outreach ministry to junior high students on Wednesday evenings that he called Campus Club. It had become more successful in a shorter time than he had imagined, because 130 high-energy balls of fire were tearing through the gymnasium and fellowship hall. Reinforcements were urgent. Don set out in desperate search of some equally high-energy college students who could corral this bunch and invest in their lives. I was on his list. "Greg, how would you like to be a part of a team of college students working with junior high kids on Wednesday nights?" That was definitely one of those moments when I didn't know enough to say no. "Sure, great. What do you want me to do?" I said.

I don't recall that the original invitation included a bonus, but a bonus I got. Don would periodically phone to see if we could get together one on one. Often the substantive portion of this time was preceded by swatting balls around the tennis court. Invariably our time would conclude with an extended side-by-side conversation as we sat on the bench next to the tennis court. Don would open his Bible and share with me something from the Word that was speaking to his life. What impressed me about Don was his transparency. He didn't hide from me the dark spots of his life, which the Scripture exposed, or the difficulty of making the appropriate changes. He made it clear that being a follower of Jesus wasn't easy but more than worth the cost involved. In those heart-to-heart talks an unspoken message was transferred to me. The message was, "If Don wants to follow Jesus, then I want to follow Jesus."

I don't recall whether Don's personal investment in me was influenced by some grand design as to how one does ministry or if Don intuitively knew that if you are going to make a difference in someone's life you have to get close to that person. But whether it was by intention or instinct, Don has served as a model for me as to the way Jesus ministered.

A generation ago I heard Charles Miller, then youth pastor at Lake Avenue Congregational Church in Pasadena, California, use a memorable phrase. He said the Scripture is not only a message book but also a method book. In other words, the Scripture conveys not only the what but also the how. We tend to look at Scripture as merely containing the content of the gospel and the commensurate lifestyle. But also imbedded in the story of the good news is instruction and modeling of the means we are to use to ensure its transmission into the lives of the next generation. My fundamental assumption is that we have less of a message problem today than we do a method problem. We have not been looking to Scripture to show us how people grow to maturity in Christ so that they can reproduce.

In this and the next two chapters we will examine the strategy that Jesus and Paul used to transmit the faith from one generation to another. We need to have the biblical perspective clearly in mind. By following the imperative of Scripture, we can work within small discipling units to carefully grow people in the faith and overcome the rampant superficiality of our age. What we will discover in the ministries of Jesus and Paul is that they staked their fruitfulness on intentional, relational investment in a few. This is the way to ensure the linkage of discipleship from one generation to the next.

DOING THE LORD'S WORK IN THE LORD'S WAY

It is estimated that four to six months into Jesus' public ministry, he selected from a larger group of followers those who would move from the category of disciples to that of apostles. Luke records this event: "Now during those days he [Jesus] went out the mountain to pray; and he spent the night in prayer to God. And when day came, he called his disciples and chose twelve of them, whom he also named apostles" (Luke 6:12-13).

One could get the impression from reading Mark's account of Jesus' call of the disciples that the call to be apostles occurred during his first encounter with them. Jesus passed by the Sea of Galilee, observed two sets of brothers, Peter and Andrew and James and John, plying their trade—fishing. He walked up to them and without introduction exclaimed, "Follow me and I will make you fish for people" (Mark 1:17). Precipitously they dropped everything and like puppies followed their new master. So mesmerized were they by Jesus' charisma that they laid down their nets after only a moment's exposure. This conjures up images of glassy-eyed, cult-like obedience to a personality-negating guru.

A closer reading of the Gospels indicates that becoming part of Jesus' inner circle progressed through stages. A. B. Bruce, in *The Training of the Twelve*, says that responding to Jesus' selection to be a part of the inner group was the third of three stages in a process.[1]

The first stage is recorded in John's Gospel. Most commentators view our introduction to the first disciples in John 1 as preceding the point where Matthew, Mark and Luke begin their Gospels. John indicates that the initial encounters with Jesus initiated a period of examination. The first disciples were invited by Jesus to check him out to see if he was the Messiah for whom they were looking. Andrew and an unnamed disciple (most likely John) were introduced to Jesus by means of John the Baptist. As disciples of John the Baptist, they had been prepared to look for the Messiah for whom John prepared the way. John, upon seeing Jesus, exclaimed, "Look, here is the Lamb of God" (John 1:36). Andrew and John take it upon themselves to follow Jesus. During this investigative stage Jesus invites them to "come and see" (John 1:39). Jesus encourages exposure to him as a way for the disciples to get a glimpse on their terms of who he might be. Also included in this time of inquiry are Peter, who is informed by Andrew, "We have found the Messiah" (John 1:41), and Philip, who uses the same phrase with a skeptical Nathaniel (likely Bartholomew), "We have found him" (John 1:45).

We are left with the clear notion that those who would later become the Twelve began as inquirers or seekers. They were not at first encounter presented with the decision, "Follow me," but instead, "Come and see." There would soon come a time when a decision would have to be made, but first the authenticity and identity of this engaging person would have a chance to leave a growing impression.

It is at the second stage that we pick up the story in Luke 6. Jesus has called together a crowd of disciples, from whom he is to select an inner core of twelve. The crowd has been gathered at Jesus' initiative. If stage one allows the inquirers to control the investigation, at stage two Jesus defines the nature of the relationship through a summons that requires a decision: "Follow me" (John 1:43; Mark 1:20; 2:14; Luke 9:59; Matthew 8:21; 19:22). Speaking to the crowds, Jesus says, "If any want to become my followers, let them deny themselves and take up their cross daily and follow me" (Luke 9:23). Jesus provides the shaping influence. The lexical definition of "disciple" (*mathētēs*) "always implies the existence of a personal attachment which shapes the whole life of the one described as *mathētēs*, and which in its particularity, leaves no doubt as to who is deploying the formative power."[2] At this stage the Twelve are part of the larger group who have responded to the specific yet corporate call to be one of Jesus' disciples. This crowd gathered by Jesus may be equivalent to the seventy whom Jesus would later send out two by two (Luke 10:1-2).

The third stage moves each of the Twelve from the category of one-among-many-disciples to a leadership role in Jesus' intimate inner circle. In other words, any follower of Jesus is a disciple, but only twelve of these disciples are apostles. Another way to say it is that all apostles are disciples, but not all disciples are apostles. This role is reserved for a chosen few. If stage one is "come and see" and stage two is "follow me," then stage three is "come and be with me."

Against this backdrop, our interest is the strategic import of Jesus' selection of the Twelve and how Jesus' focus on a few serves as a model for how we are to grow disciples and, subsequently, leaders. The selection of the Twelve was evidently a crucial moment in Jesus' ministry. Luke underscores the pivotal nature of this selection by telling us that Jesus spent all night in prayer. So vital was this moment to the future of Jesus' ministry that extended and intense time alone with his Father preceded the call. We can only speculate as to what was on Jesus' heart that night. Was he attempting to discern who should make the final cut? Had Jesus whittled down the list to fifteen and was in a quandary as to which three to eliminate? Probably not. My best guess is that Jesus was not so much trying to settle on the right ones as he was praying that they would become the right ones. Perhaps Jesus projected each of the Twelve on the screen of his imagination, visualizing what they would become under his tutelage. Jesus saw these disciples not only as unformed lumps of coal but, under his formative and loving pressure, as the diamonds that they would become. Jesus knew full well that Peter would brashly oppose his self-designation as a suffering Messiah and would vehemently deny him. Yet Jesus envisioned by faith in the present that Peter would become the "rock" upon whom he would build his church (Matthew 16:18).

THE STRATEGIC QUESTION

Not only does Jesus' all-night prayer raise the level of the strategic significance of the choosing of the Twelve, but so does that manner in which the selection was made. Luke tells us, "He called his disciples [together] and chose twelve of them" (Luke 6:13). In other words, from the larger group Jesus called those who would be part of his inner circle. This reminds me of my elementary school days on the playground when the two most popular kids would serve as the opposing captains for the pick-up games. Those of us clamoring to play stood around the two team captains waiting for our names to be called. To hear one's name called first made you feel not only special but also a bit arrogant. You could then stand next to the team captain as one of the in crowd and suggest who should be next to be chosen. By making his selection process a public event, Jesus potentially set up a dynamic in which a few felt special and the rest felt left out. Why would Jesus create an atmosphere that would foster jealousy on the part of those not chosen and potential pride in those who were?

I hear objections from pastors who say they can't have a few in whom they invest because they will be accused of having favorites. If the pastor spends more intensive time with a few, a buzz spreads throughout the church that the pastor has his or her inner circle. From the congregation's perspective the pastor must be equally available to all. These suspicions are rooted in two assumptions. The first assumption is that the pastor's primary role after preaching is to be a caregiver. Ministry is equated with taking care of the needs of the flock. To the shepherd, the sheep must all be of equal value.

The second assumption revolves around an appropriate concern about the abuse of power. A perception can grow within a congregation that a small group controls what happens in the life of a church or ministry. Church members can then see themselves as outsiders who find it difficult to penetrate the invisible barrier of an undetectable inner circle. The egalitarian model of equal access, however, is rooted in a fundamental misunderstanding of the pastoral role. In the biblical view, pastors are gifts to the church, and they are to equip the saints for their ministry, not to minister on behalf of the saints. Just so, Jesus thought that investing in a few was so important that he made the selection process public, even at the risk stirring up jealousy and pride.

What was so important about having a few in his inner circle that Jesus was willing risk the dynamics of jealously? What were the strategic reasons behind this selection of the Twelve to be his intimate associates? Of the many valid reasons for Jesus' investment in a few, two of them seem most directly related to Jesus' goal of making self-initiating, reproducing, fully devoted followers: internalization and multiplication.

INTERNALIZATION

The only way for Jesus to grow flawed and faithless common people into mature disciples and make sure that his kingdom would transcend his earthly ministry was to have a core who knew in depth his person and mission. His life and mission needed to be internalized[3] in the lives of the disciples. The way to ensure that they internalized his mission was through "purposeful proximity."[4]

But, we might object, if Jesus was trying to reach as many as possible, why not allow the crowds and his popularity to grow so that the entourage became a mass movement? Jesus was so popular that the religious leaders dared not arrest him in public. There were times when the crush of the crowds threatened his well-being to the point where he needed to get into a boat and address the populace from just off shore. Why not stake his future on his popularity?

In fact, what we see in Jesus is a healthy and appropriate skepticism of the masses. Jesus was well aware of the crowd's ignoble motives for following him. John gives an insight into Jesus' understanding of human nature: "When he [Jesus] was in Jerusalem during the Passover festival, many believed in his name because they saw the signs that he was doing. But Jesus on his part would not entrust himself to them, because he knew all people and needed no one to testify about anyone; for he himself know what was in everyone" (John 2:23-25). The implication of John's words is that people will flock to demonstrations of power, especially if they are the beneficiaries of that power. The desperate came and received healing. Others came to be around the miracle worker. Like moths attracted to a light bulb, people are fascinated and feel alive in the presence of a charismatic, life-giving figure. Yet Jesus knew that those who clamored to be near were fickle. As soon as the demands of discipleship were to be articulated, his fan club would dwindle.

The very nature of a crowd is the ability to be lost in it. It costs nothing to be a part of the masses. One can either be positively or negatively inclined. A member of a crowd, such as a worshiper in a congregation, can remain lost in the sea of faces, neither having to commit nor declare loyalty. A person can be anything from a curious observer to a skeptic or bored pew-sitter. Jesus ministered to the crowd in order to call people out of it. One was not on the road to discipleship unless that person came out of the crowd to identify with Jesus. There are twin prerequisites for following Christ—cost and commitment, neither of which can occur in the anonymity of the masses.

What would have been the outcome if Jesus had staked the future of his ministry on the loyalty of the crowds? We know the answer to that because we are given a window into the dramatic turnaround of the populace at large. Jesus' popularity publicly reached a crescendo on the day we call Palm Sunday. Jesus rode into Jerusalem amid the adoration of those waiting for their military messiah. Coats and palm branches created a pathway upon which Jesus' donkey trod. The city was filled with shouts of "Hosanna, glory to God in the highest." Yet in five days the same mouths that sang out "Hosanna" would howl "Crucify him, crucify him." This turning is why Bruce wrote, "But for the twelve, the doctrine, the works, the image of Jesus might have perished from human resemblance, nothing remaining but a vague mythical tradition, of historical value, of little practical importance."[5]

In spite of Jesus' clear strategy of calling people from the crowds and focusing on a few, we continue to rely on preaching and programs as the means to make disciples. If we rely on the teaching content of preaching to fuel discipleship, then we have a misplaced confidence. Discipleship is fundamentally a relational process. Preaching can be a solitary one. The worshiper tends to be an isolated, passive recipient of the preached word. Preaching at its best calls people to become a disciple by pointing people to disciple-making settings, such as reproducible, discipling relationships.

Second, as I indicated in chapter one, we have relied on programs to make disciples. We rely on programs because we don't want to pay the price of personal investment that discipleship requires. By putting people through programs, we foolishly hope that we can mass produce disciples. Leroy Eims critiques this approach incisively when he writes, "Disciples cannot be mass produced. We cannot drop people into a program and see disciples emerge at the end of the production line. It takes time to make disciples. It takes individual personal attention."[6]

Jesus knew that he had to get beyond the superficial and prioritize a few if disciples were to made. This required that his disciples have consistent, continuous exposure to his life, so that in the context of honest and open interchange, he could speak to the real stuff of their lives. When the disciples argued over who was the greatest, he was able to turn their value system on its head by insisting that in his kingdom the greatest are the least. Peter revealed his working model of a messiah when he told Jesus that no messiah of his was going to die at the hands of the religious leaders. Jesus immediately rebuked Peter for being nothing less than the mouthpiece of Satan. On numerous occasions Jesus' public teaching was followed by a private tutorial for the disciples. The disciples had the opportunity to ask for an explanation of the meaning of Jesus' words, and Jesus had the opportunity to speak to the implications for their lives in a way that could never be conveyed to the crowds.

I have often wondered why Jesus didn't employ the usual means of preserving his legacy. We have nothing penned by his hand. He seemed unconcerned about official manuscripts or enlisting a scribe who could record all of his teachings. It is standard practice that when presidents leave office, they open a presidential library to preserve and display the significant documents from their administration and media moments. A former president attempts to shape the perceptions of history by writing his memoirs. Why did Jesus not choose the same approach? Jesus appeared to rely on two means to carry his life and mission forward: the Holy Spirit and the Twelve. His life was transferred to their life by his Spirit and by his association with and investment in them. The irrefutable legacy Jesus wanted to leave behind was the transformed lives of ordinary men who would carry on his work after he returned to the Father. Internalization occurred through intense association.

Bruce draws the summary conclusion, "This careful, painstaking education of the disciples secured [that] the teacher's influence should be permanent; that His kingdom should be founded on deep and indestructible convictions in the minds of a few, not on the shifting sands of *superficial* impressions in the minds of the many."[7]

The first strategic reason for Jesus' focus on a few was to ensure the internalization of his life and ministry in those who would be the foundation of the Jesus movement.

MULTIPLICATION

With Jesus' focus on the Twelve, one might conclude that Jesus was unconcerned about the multitudes. Jim Egli and Paul Zehr, in their study of the Gospel of Mark, found that Jesus spent 49 percent of his time with the disciples, and even more time as he set his face toward Jerusalem and the cross.[8] Is this not further evidence that the masses were receding from his field of vision? Absolutely not! Jesus did not think like we do. We think we need to put on events that draw crowds to reach the multitudes. We equate vision with the size of our audience. Jesus had vision of another sort. Jesus had enough vision to think small. Indeed, it was because of his compassion for the harassed and harried throng that Jesus gave himself to the Twelve. Eugene Peterson's humorous overstatement puts this in perspective: "Jesus, it must be remembered, restricted nine-tenths of his ministry to twelve Jews because it was the only way to redeem all Americans."[9]

The irony is that in our attempt to reach the masses through mass means we have failed to train people the masses could emulate. We often perpetuate superficiality by casting a wider net, without the commensurate depth. Jesus multiplied his life in the Twelve so that there would be more of himself to go around. In the mid-1970s the movie *Jesus Christ Superstar* stirred controversy because of its portrayal of a very human Christ confused about his mission. While the theology of the film left much to be desired, one powerful scene left a deep impression on me. In this scene Jesus is a solitary figure standing on the slope of barren, scraggly desert hillside. As Jesus sings a song of pathos, black slinky figures emerge from the pockmarked crevices. Each figure represents an aspect of the world's darkness. As the Christ figure sings emotively about man's inhumanity to man, crushing poverty, incurable disease and the great enemy death, these black slithery beings envelop Jesus one at a time until he is crushed and covered by the darkness. The viewer is left with the question, How can one person take on and bear all of this darkness alone? Of course, on the most fundamental level we believe that Jesus did bear it all as the solitary substitute for the guilt of our sin through his death on the cross. Yet there is a sense in which Jesus did not intend to bear it all. By investing in a few, Jesus intended to transfer his life to others, so that they would be about this business of extending his redemptive life to the multitudes.

Robert Coleman writes, "The initial objective of Jesus' plan was to enlist men who could bear witness to his life and carry on His work after He returned to His father."[10] George Martin takes Jesus' strategy and challenges pastors to apply it to the way they think about ministry today:

> Perhaps today's pastor should imagine that they are going to have three more years in their parish (church) as pastor—that there will be no replacement for them when they leave. If they acted as if this were going to happen, they would put the highest priority on selecting, motivating, and training lay leaders that could carry on as much as possible the mission of the parish after they left. The results of three sustained years of such an approach would be significant. Even revolutionary.[11]

As a part of my workshop on discipleship, I enjoy a playful exercise in which I invite the participants to implement Martin's challenge. Generally 80 to 90 percent of the participants are key lay leaders in their congregation, with the paid staff scattered among them. Their assignment is to rewrite the job descriptions of the paid staff, knowing that they had only three years left in their ministry and no one to replace them. I say, "Here's your chance. You have always wanted to tell your pastors what to do." The responses of lay leaders are perceptive. They immediately realize that there must be a radical shift in priorities. There are many things their paid staff must cease doing if they are to leave behind self-initiating, reproducing, fully devoted followers of Jesus. Usually the list of things that others could do includes caregiving responsibilities, various aspects of administration and attendance at committee meetings. In place of these unfocused activities could be intentional discipling relationships; specific leadership training on topics such as preaching, spiritual oversight, evangelism and small group leadership; and careful study of the Word, so that teaching could be in greater depth.

Jesus lived with the urgency of the three-year timeline. With the cross before him, he knew that he had to prepare the Twelve to carry on his mission. Each day meant he was closer to the reason for which he came to this earth, and therefore a day closer to the time when his ministry would become theirs. Jesus' strategy was to expand the leadership base so that instead of there being one of him, there would be twelve (knowing even that one of them would be lost). Mark's account of the selection of the Twelve makes it clear that Jesus intended his ministry to become theirs. "He went up the mountain and called to him those whom he wanted, and they came to him. And he appointed twelve, whom he also named apostles, to be with him, and to be sent out to proclaim the message, and to have authority to cast out demons" (Mark 3:13-15).

The same message that Jesus proclaimed was transferred to the lips of the apostles. Jesus declared the arrival of the kingdom of God in his person. Just so, the apostles announced from village to village that the future reign of God that was to bring in the glorious age had broken into this present darkness. The popular Jewish apocalyptic was that this age would be replaced at the coming of the Messiah with the age to come. The kingdom of God was envisioned in political terms. A political ruler like David would reestablish the glory days of Israel by liberating it from the Roman oppressor. Jesus instead pictured the reign of God as a spiritual invasion that would first liberate the hearts of people from the imprisonment of sin. A new, otherworldly order had come alongside and was supplanting the ruler of this age. The apostles were given authority to release people from demons as a sign that the kingdom of God was penetrating the darkness. The message of the kingdom was confirmed in power by the signs of the kingdom. Jesus was now extending himself into the lives of the Twelve, who were being prepared in Jesus' presence to carry on in his absence.

Jesus' strategy illustrates a principle that church leaders witness regularly: The reach of our ministries is directly proportional to the breadth of our leadership base. Only to the extent that we have grown self-initiating, reproducing, fully devoted disciples can new ministries touch the brokenness of people's lives. Therefore we see unmet needs because we have not intentionally grown champions to meet those needs. However, Jesus knew the human limitation of his incarnate state. As a solitary human being his reach was limited. His strategy was designed to touch the whole world through the multiplication of disciples who were carefully trained. On the eve of his date with the cross, he saw how much fruit his deliberate strategy of multiplication would bear. He said to his disciples, "Very truly, I tell you, the one who believes in me will also do the works that I do and, in fact, will do greater works than these, because I am going to the Father" (John 14:12). How can it be that someone could do greater works than the Son of God? The "greater works" were most likely a matter of quantity more than quality. By Jesus' multiplication of himself in the Twelve, they would geographically cover far greater territory than he ever did in his limited itinerant ministry. By the power of the indwelling Holy Spirit carrying them to the entire known world, the sheer volume of Jesus' ministry would expand exponentially. And so it has been.

By focusing on a few, Jesus was not displaying indifference to the multitudes. Instead, Jesus had a different vision for reaching the masses than our approach through mass gatherings. Jesus had enough vision to think small. Robert Coleman captured Jesus' methodology with the turn of a phrase: "Jesus' concern was not with programs to reach the multitudes, but with men the multitudes would follow."[12] After internalization, multiplication was the second strategic reason why Jesus focused on a few.

THE ABSENCE OF INTENTIONAL DISCIPLING

Jesus focused on a few because that was the way to grow people and ensure transference of his heart and vision to them. This kind of relationship, however, has been lacking in many of our lives.

Much of my passion for intentional discipling comes from not wanting others to experience what happened to me. It is true that our deepest convictions come from our life experience. As a fearful, emotionally burdened seventh grader, with only tentative connections to the church, I responded to the invitation to attend a weekend church camp. I heard exactly what I needed that weekend. The preacher on Saturday wrapped up his message with Jesus' words and summons, "Come to me, all you that are weary and are carrying heavy burdens, and I will give you rest" (Matthew 11:28).

When the invitation came to receive Christ, I wanted what Jesus had to offer—rest. Putting my trust in Christ opened the floodgates, for oceans of love seemed to roll over me. That evening our camp counselor asked if anyone had something to share from the day's events. After some awkward silence I timidly raised my hand and volunteered my encounter with the living Christ. I remember being handed a decision card, which I completed and returned to my counselor. I recall receiving only the barest of guidance about what I should do now that I had this life-altering connection to Christ. I made a valiant effort to read my Bible daily upon returning home, because, I suppose, someone said that might be a good thing.

In retrospect, I thought that I might hear from someone from the church, since I had turned in the decision card. I heard from no one. The silence was resounding. As a shy seventh grader, it never occurred to me to go to someone in the know and say, "Okay, now what? How do I go about growing in this newfound love in my life?" Instead, I drifted for years, grateful that I had a companion in Jesus that I had not had before, but I had no idea of what to do next.

This should never be! I lost a number of years when my heart was ripe to be nurtured in this new faith. Yes, Jesus has been gracious to hold onto to me in spite of the human failure and providentially brought people into my life in my latter high school and college years who would engage me in a discipleship process, but the church did not serve as a disciple-making body. If making disciples is the mission of the church, why are churches generally not prepared to provide the nurturing environment that grows self-initiating, reproducing, fully devoted followers of Jesus?

We could close the discipleship gap if we adopted Jesus' approach to making self-initiating, reproducing, fully devoted followers. By investing in a few over a three-year period, Jesus was able to internalize his message and mission into his disciples. I was fortunate during my college years to have someone like Don make up for what I had not received in my stumbling start with Christ. Don's open heart and his generosity with his time effected transference through close association. Don's passion for Christ infected this disciple, and multiplication took place. When Don graduated from seminary, the junior high ministry was suddenly without its leader, but it was not without leadership. Don had left himself behind in me and others. The church staff invited me to continue what Don had started. For two summers during my college years I led the junior high ministry with my college peers. Don had prepared us for his departure.

We now turn our emphasis from the strategic reasons for Jesus investing in a few to the way that Jesus went about preparing the disciples to carry on his mission after he returned to the Father. Jesus brought his disciples through a process of growth to the intended outcome, which was to carry on his mission. They went from clueless to complete in three years. How did Jesus do that?

4

Jesus' Preparatory Empowerment Model

In chapter three we examined two strategic reasons for Jesus' selection of the Twelve—internalization and multiplication. Jesus focused on a few because that was the only way to transplant his heart and mission into the lives of his key followers. Internalization cannot happen through a mass transference to an audience, but must occur in an interpersonal environment. True multiplication or reproduction is possible only when disciples so internalize the mission that they are motivated to pass it on to others. Robert Coleman has written, "The best work is always done with a few. Better to give a year or so to one or two men who learn what it means to conquer for Christ than to spend a lifetime with a congregation just keeping the program going."[1]

Coleman's comment leads us to the focus of this chapter. How did Jesus go about shaping and training the Twelve to become fishers of people? Did Jesus open a school? Did he offer semester courses in which the disciples could enroll? Was there the carrot of a diploma, a certificate of apostleship that gave them the credentials to be apostles of Jesus? Did he appoint himself as chancellor of Jesus University? Was there a curriculum that Jesus wanted his students to master?

As important as Jesus' teaching was, it was his person that became the vehicle for the transmission of his life to his disciples. David Watson draws into sharp focus the centrality of the person of Jesus: "When Buddha was dying, his disciples asked how they could best remember him. He told them not to bother; it was his teaching, not his person, that counted. With Jesus it was altogether different. Everything centers on *him,* his person. Discipleship means knowing *him,* loving *him,* believing in *him,* being committed to *him.*"[2] The message was enfleshed and inseparable from who he was. "Jesus' leadership development of his under-shepherds was not so much a course or a curriculum as it was a shared life?"[3]

Living on this side of Pentecost, it is easy to forget where Jesus had to begin with the Twelve. Who were these apostles that Jesus selected to walk with him? With what did Jesus have to work? Were they made out of superior stuff that gave them the innate ability to accomplish extraordinary things? It is a sobering fact that Jesus selected ordinary, plain-vanilla people who were no different from you or me. This is brought home in a humorous way by an apocryphal memorandum spoofing the usual way people are screened for professional ministry today (see page 77).[4]

It has been broadly observed that the disciples were the rawest of raw material when Jesus first got ahold of them. "They were poor men of humble birth, low station, mean occupations, who had never felt the stimulating influence of a liberal education, or of social intercourse with persons of cultivated minds."[5] They were not the kind of people who would give instant credibility to Jesus' ministry. In our day, when people want to start a new enterprise, they seek to assure their future constituents by lining their letterhead with names that inspire confidence. It would hardly have been reassuring for the Palestinian investor in this new venture to read, "Peter and Andrew, James and John, fishermen; Matthew, tax

---

Memorandum

TO:
Jesus, Son of Joseph
Woodcrafter Carpenter Shop
Nazareth

FROM:
Jordan Management Consultants
Jerusalem

Dear Sir:
Thank you for submitting the resumes of the twelve men you have picked for management positions in your new organization. All of them have now taken our battery of tests; we have not only run the results through our computer but also arranged personal interviews for each of them with our psychologist and vocational aptitude consultant.

It is the staff opinion that most of your nominees are lacking in background, education and vocational aptitude for the type of enterprise you are undertaking. They do not have the team concept. We would recommend that you continue your search for persons of experience in managerial ability and proven capability.

Simon Peter is emotionally unstable and given to fits of temper. Andrew has absolutely no qualities of leadership. The two brothers, James and John, the sons of Zebedee, place personal interest above company loyalty. Thomas demonstrates a questioning attitude that would tend to undermine morale.

We feel that it is our duty to tell you that Matthew has been blacklisted by the Greater Jerusalem Better Business Bureau. James, the son of Alphaeus, and Thaddaeus definitely have radical leanings, and they both registered a high score on the manic-depressive scale.

One of the candidates, however, shows great potential. He is a man of ability and resourcefulness, meets people well, has a keen business mind and has contacts in high places. He is highly motivated, ambitious and responsible. We recommend Judas Iscariot as your controller and right-hand man. All of the other profiles are self-explanatory.

We wish you every success in your new venture.

Sincerely yours,
Jordan Management Consultants

---

collector; Simon, religious zealot." The Twelve, with the exception of Judas Iscariot, were hicks from the hill country of Galilee whose accents would show that they were "uneducated and ordinary men" (Acts 4:13).

Not only did they not have privileged birth, positions of power in the religious establishment or an education that would qualify them to be legal scholars, they came with all the foibles of their day. "At the time of their call they were exceedingly ignorant, narrow-minded, superstitious, full of Jewish prejudices, misconceptions, and animosities. They had much to unlearn of what was bad, as well as much to learn of what was good, and they were both slow to learn and unlearn."[6] The disciples were products of their time with all its limitations, as in any age. They had absorbed the common view that women were not worthy to be taught the Torah. In one incident Jesus remained at Jacob's well in Samaria speaking to a questionable woman, while the disciples went to a nearby village to purchase food. Upon their return the disciples "were astonished that he was speaking with a woman" (John 4:27). For the disciples, speaking to a woman was even more scandalous than speaking to a despised Samaritan. Then there's James and John, who drew the ire of their ten companions when they were caught trying to out-maneuver the others for positions of power when Jesus came into his kingdom. I have not even mentioned Peter, the disciple without an unexpressed thought. When Jesus called the Twelve, they were a reclamation project of the first order. Just like us.

Yet their association with Jesus over a three-year period served to transform this ragtag group into world-beaters. After the de-scent of the promised Holy Spirit at Pentecost, a group of fright-ened, cowardly disciples was transformed into fearless mega-phones for the resurrected Christ. Two of the disciples, Peter and John, were arrested by the religious leaders and told to cease tell-ing people that Jesus was alive. Respectfully Peter and John de-clined to succumb to this pressure, instead stating that "there is salvation in no one else, for there is no other name under heaven given among mortals by which we must be saved" (Acts 4:12). Then we find this reluctant commendation in the text regarding Peter and John: "Now when they saw the boldness of Peter and John and realized that they were uneducated and ordinary men, they were amazed and recognized them as companions of Jesus" (Acts 4:13).

This leads us back to the burden of this chapter. How did Jesus set about shaping these twelve into people prepared to carry on his work after he returned the Father? Acts 4:13 echoes Mark's version of the call of the Twelve to be apostles: "And he appointed twelve, whom he also named apostles, to be with him" (Mark 3:14). Being with Jesus in a relational setting served as the basis to shape the disciples' character and instill Jesus' mission in them.

What was the relational, developmental process that Jesus took these disciples through so that they would be ready to carry on his mission? At the outset we must acknowledge that there is no clear, step-by-step formula outlined in the Gospels. Attempts have been made to fit the gospel content into distinct phases, as if Jesus were operating out of a sequential leadership development model. Though I will describe a developmental process through which the disciples progressed, the stages were overlapping and repetitive. Human beings grow, fall back, relearn, stumble forward, lose their way, get back on track. Our growth process is somewhat like a sine wave on a gradual uphill course, taking a person in zigzag fashion to a higher level. It is often only in retrospect that we realize progress is being made. Martin Luther King Jr. used to close many of his talks with the old slave's prayer: " O God, I ain't what I ought to be and I ain't what I'm gonna be, but thanks be to you, I ain't what I used to be."[7]

PRE-DISCIPLE (INQUIRY) STAGE

Before I outline the developmental stages through which Jesus brought the disciples, it is important to acknowledge that a hard line must be crossed to enter into this growth process. There is no formation without submission. In the pre-disciple phase, described as stage one in the previous chapter (see pages 61-62), the disciples control their inquiry. We noted in John 1 that Andrew and the "other" disciple tag along after Jesus when he comes on the scene. Jesus says to them, "What are you looking for?" (John 1:38). The two indicate that they want some time with Jesus in order to satisfy themselves that Jesus is the promised One. Jesus says simply, "Come and see." They are the investigators, and Jesus is the subject.

But in order for discipleship to occur, the tables must be turned. The seeking ones must become the submitted ones. The bold line between "come and see" and "come and follow me" must be crossed. Only then does Jesus exercise his shaping influence over their lives. This is where Jesus pulls the great reversal on the accepted way that disciples attached to a rabbi. The standard practice was that disciples investigated various rabbis and decided to whom they wanted to attach themselves. In other words, the disciples controlled their destinies. Not so with Jesus. Michael Wilkins observes, "Whereas discipleship was a voluntary initiative with other types of master-disciple relationships in the first century, with Jesus the initiative lay with his choice and call of those who would be his disciples."[8] Up to this point, Andrew (and John) were like any other disciples seeking a rabbi. Soon the tables would be turned, and Jesus would issue the call, "Come and follow me," which required a yes or no. This concept is integral to the nature of discipleship. Jesus is the one who must be in the lead position on his terms.

Once this line had been crossed, Jesus led the disciples through a four-stage preparatory process (see figure 4.1). Two insights from a popular leadership model helped open my eyes to Jesus' growth process with the disciples. Paul Hersey and Ken Blanchard, in *Situational Leadership,* state that good leaders do two things.

First, they have a readiness goal in mind for their followers. Second, they adjust their leadership style to the level of preparedness of an individual or group in order to progress toward the readiness goal. Hersey and Blanchard define readiness as "the ability and willingness of a person or group to take responsibility for directing their own behavior."[9] Their theory is that there is no one best or right style of leadership, but one's style must be adapted to fit the readiness level of those they are helping to reach the goal.

In the same way, Jesus called his disciples "to be with him" with the readiness goal of carrying on in his absence. "He knew what they could not see, that He had chosen them in order to train them as the future leaders in the church and mission field, for the day that He would leave them."[10] Jesus had a clear goal to be reached in three years. In chapter three we reflected on George Martin's three-year challenge: What difference would it make in the way we, as leaders, spent our time if we knew that we had only three years remaining in our current ministry and there would be no leaders to replace us? Jesus lived with this sense of destiny. He was on a short timetable and had to bring his replacements to a state of readiness. What was Jesus' readiness goal? Jesus' goal was that the disciples would assume full responsibility for being and making self-initiating, reproducing, fully devoted followers. But to do that he had to begin where they were and carefully shape them through a preparatory development process. What was that process?

Jesus acted as a master trainer. His life destiny was the cross. He was the man born to die. Yet converging on that moment would be the necessity of having his disciples prepared to carry on his mission after his resurrection and return to the Father. To get the disciples ready, Jesus played a series of important roles, commensurate with the disciples' preparedness. At stage one, early in his ministry, Jesus was a living example. The disciples watched him carefully and therefore began to absorb his message and his ministry. At stage two, Jesus was a provocative educator. Jesus' intent was not

	PRE-DISCIPLE	STAGE 1	STAGE 2	STAGE 3	STAGE 4
Jesus' role	The inviter	The living example	The provocative teacher	The supportive coach	The ultimate delegator
The disciples' role	Seekers	Observers and imitators	Students and questioners	Short-term missionaries	Apostles
Readiness level	Hungry to know whether Jesus was the long-awaited Messiah	Ready to observe who Jesus is and the nature of his ministry and mission	Ready to interact with Jesus and publicly identify with him	Ready to test the authority of Jesus to work through them	Ready to assume full responsibility for making reproducing disciples
Key questions	Is Jesus the Messiah?	Who is Jesus, and what is his ministry and mission?	What is the cost of following Jesus?	Will the power of Jesus work through us when we take on his ministry?	Will I give my life entirely to the mission of making reproducing disciples?

Figure 4.1. Jesus' preparatory empowerment process

only to inform the disciples of a new kingdom perspective but also to dislodge the wrong-headed ideas and assumptions that they had picked up from a religious and secular world in rebellion against God. At stage three, Jesus was a supportive coach. The disciples were sent on a short-term mission within Jesus' clear parameters, knowing that he was there for a supportive debriefing upon their return. At stage four, Jesus was the ultimate delegator. The disciples had internalized enough to survive their scattering at Jesus' crucifixion, to be regrouped after the resurrection and empowered by the Holy Spirit at Pentecost. His ministry had become theirs.

DEVELOPMENTAL STAGE ONE:
JESUS, THE LIVING EXAMPLE

At this first stage of their development, the disciples needed to comprehend the nature of Jesus' ministry and mission and to ask the all-important question, Who is this person who says and does such phenomenal things? In the initial stages of training, the leader needs to be highly directive. The leader sets the agenda and defines the roles of the neophytes. For Jesus this meant that he presented himself as the living example for the disciples to observe and study. "Knowledge was gained by association before it was understood by explanation."[11] The sentence "I do, you watch" describes this stage.

It appears that early in Jesus' ministry the role of disciples was to be quiet observers. The disciples are present at the various encounters or teachings of Jesus, but they have receded into the background. One has the sense that they are standing off to the side, observing Jesus in action. He is the focus. "This was the essence of his training program—just letting his disciples follow him."[12] Jesus' approach was similar to the role of a rabbi in the life of a student. In the rabbinic model a disciple literally copied a life. Rabbis were considered to be the living Torah—the rule of life with skin on. Referring to the rabbinical approach, Gerhardsson writes,

"To learn one must go to a Teacher. . . . But they also learn a great deal by simply observing: with attentive eyes they observe all that the teacher does and then proceed to imitate him. Torah is above all a holy, authoritative attitude towards life and way of life. Because this is true, much can be learned simply by watching and imitating those who are learned."[13]

Let's take one portion of the Gospels and look at them from the standpoint of the disciples' role. In the first five chapters of the Gospel of Mark, the disciples are mentioned only sporadically—just enough to let us know that they are present. Mark highlights three emphases about the person of Jesus that the disciples observe. First, Mark establishes Jesus' authority over the demonic (Mark 1:21-28; 5:1-20), over sin (Mark 2:1-12), over the sabbath (Mark 2:23—3:6); over nature (Mark 4:35-41), over illness and disease (Mark 1:40-45; 5:21-34) and even over death (5:35-43).

Second, Mark paints a picture of the people for whom Jesus has a heart: the demoniacs (Mark 1:23; 5:2), the leper (Mark 1:40), the paralyzed man on a pallet (Mark 2:3), Levi the tax collector (Mark 2:14), a man with a withered hand (Mark 3:1), a hemorrhaging woman (Mark 5:25), and a ruler of the synagogue and his daughter ill unto death (Mark 5:41).

Third, Mark dramatizes the religious establishment's antagonism toward Jesus. The Pharisees mock Jesus' authority to forgive the paralytic (Mark 2:6-7), disdain his eating with tax collectors and sinners (Mark 2:16), are shocked that he and his disciples violate the sabbath (Mark 2:24), watch in wait for him to heal on the sabbath (Mark 3:2) and declare that Jesus is demon possessed (Mark 3:22).

Where are the disciples as Jesus establishes his authority over the forces of evil, his heart for the outcast and his antagonism toward the religious establishment? They are essentially taking this all in. What appearances do the disciples make in the first five chapters of Mark? Beyond the four fishermen responding to the call to follow Jesus, the disciples appear in the form of "they" when Jesus enters the synagogue in Capernaum and delivers a man with an unclean spirit (Mark 1:21-28) and at the home of Andrew and Peter, where Jesus heals Peter's mother-in-law (Mark 1:29-31). Peter and the others next appear in their frantic search for Jesus, who has slipped away to a "deserted place" to be with his Father (Mark 1:35-39). Otherwise they receive only brief mention. They are dinner guests in the home of Levi, the tax collector (Mark 2:15-17). They became an issue because they are not fasting, while John the Baptist's and the Pharisees' disciples fast (Mark 2:18). They are a source of controversy since they plucked heads of grain from the fields on the sabbath (Mark 2:23-28). In Mark 3 there is the definitive moment when Jesus chooses the twelve who were to be his apostles (Mark 3:13-15). Yet Jesus seems to be in no particular hurry at this time for them to enter into this mission, since there is a considerable delay between their designation as apostles and their being sent out by Jesus. In Mark 4 the disciples' fear is aroused by the storm that threatens their lives and replaced by an even greater fear once Jesus commands the storm to cease. The last appearance of the disciples in the first five chapters of Mark is the triad of Peter, James and John, who are present when Jesus raises Jairus's daughter.

The disciples' only substantive interaction with Jesus in the first five chapters of Mark occurs after Jesus' public teaching on the parable of the soils. Otherwise the disciples tag along. But they are not nonentities. The telling question is the one the disciples ask after Jesus stills the storm: "Who then is this, that even the wind and the sea obey him?" (Mark 4:41). In the observe/imitate stage, this issue predominates: Who is this man? Who does he think he is? The fascination with the person of Jesus forms the basis for discipleship.

Even though this may be the foundational stage of discipleship, observation/imitation continues as a means of formation throughout Jesus' ministry. Just prior to his crucifixion, Jesus kneels before each of them to wash their feet, as a household servant would do for an invited guest. Even here at the end of Jesus' earthly ministry, the disciples still have not grasped that greatness is measured by descent, not ascent. Jesus has to go beyond verbal instruction to modeling. After washing the feet of each of the disciples, he draws the incident to a close by making explicit the point of his action: "So if I, your Lord and Teacher, have washed your feet, you also ought to wash one another's feet. For I have set you an example, that you also should do as I have done to you" (John 13:14-15).

Jesus stated this principle explicitly when he said, "A disciple is not above the teacher, but everyone who is fully qualified will be like the teacher" (Luke 6:40). At the most basic level, a disciple is simply a learner. The first level of learning is the desire to be like a model. Jesus is saying that discipleship training is not about information transfer, from head to head, but imitation, life to life.

My wife is an elementary school principal. Prior to her career as a principal she earned her spurs by teaching at almost every elementary school grade level. Over her career, spanning almost three decades, she has witnessed numerous advances in educational theory and technology. The classroom has become a much more stimulating place to be. There is no need for a child to be bored, for there are many ways to learn. Yet she constantly reminds me that one thing has not changed and never will change: the people factor. The most important ingredient in motivating a child to learn is the bond between the teacher and the student. The old expression is still quite true: "People don't care how much you know until they know how much you care."

The magnetic attraction of the life and ministry of Jesus became the focus of the disciples in this initial stage.

DEVELOPMENTAL STAGE TWO: JESUS, THE PROVOCATIVE TEACHER

It is fascinating to watch Jesus' leadership style vary in relationship to the readiness of his followers. Jesus, though, was not just responding to the disciples' readiness level. Jesus intentionally changed his leadership style in order to provoke the apostles to a new stage of readiness as well. At this second stage, Jesus acts as a provocative teacher. Jesus instructs or questions his apostles apart from the crowds in order to confound them and cause them to rethink their basic worldview. Jesus continues to lead in these moments, but he draws the disciples into interaction so that they can assess what it will take to be a follower of Jesus. This stage can be described by the sentence "I do, you help."

Jesus' teaching of the disciples occurred in his ministry. Class was always in session. As Jesus went about his ministry of teaching, preaching and healing, he was conscious that these settings served as training events for the few. First the disciples heard or observed Jesus in his public ministry, and then with regularity Jesus turned to them to offer further explanation or pose questions.

Let's examine two instructive moments when Jesus turned from either teaching the crowds or engaging in dialogue in order to interact with his disciples. Just as a would-be disciple today begins a relationship with Jesus with a host of half-truths, misguided thoughts, and lies, so did the Twelve. These interactions are intended to unmask and confront those attitudes and values that are not in line with Jesus' kingdom perspective. For the disciples these were gut-check times, when they had to assess the cost and commitment necessary to identify with Jesus. They had their cherished assumptions and worldviews challenged to the core.

The first incident, found in Mark 7, records Jesus' confrontation with the scribes and Pharisees over a difference of opinion about the nature of righteousness. To the religious leaders, righteousness was equated with outward behavior, such as ritual washing of hands prior to touching food. To Jesus, righteousness was first and foremost a matter of heart. Jesus summarized his position, "Then he called the crowd again and said to them, 'Listen to me, all of you, and understand: there is nothing outside a person that by going in can defile, but the things that come out are what defile'" (Mark 7:14-15). At this point Jesus makes a deliberate shift from the public to a private moment: "When he had left the crowd and entered the house, his disciples asked him about the parable" (Mark 7:17). Jesus drives home his point with pressing questions: "Then do you also fail to understand? Do you not see that whatever goes into a person from outside cannot defile, since it enters, not the heart but the stomach, and goes out into the sewer?" (Mark 7:18-19). The disciples were not quick to get Jesus' point, because they had a view of righteousness more akin to that of their religious leaders, since their teaching would have predominated. Only in these private moments could Jesus reframe their understanding of truth.

A second encounter in Mark 10 becomes another occasion in which Jesus corrects the theological myths that the disciples have absorbed. A man we have come to know as the "rich young ruler" approaches Jesus. Here is a great catch, if he can be reeled in. The young man seems eager enough. "Good Teacher, what must I do to inherit eternal life?" (Mark 10:17). Jesus responds with a mysterious retort, "Why do you call me good?"[14] In response to what he must do, Jesus enumerates some of the Ten Commandments. Upon hearing these, the rich young ruler pronounces himself spotless. But Jesus doesn't accept his self-justification. He exposes his god: "You lack one thing; go, sell what you own . . . then come, follow me" (Mark 10:21). Jesus calls the question. The young ruler walks away grieving because of his attachment to his great wealth.

Immediately Jesus swivels toward the disciples and draws the conclusion, "How hard it will be for those who have wealth to enter the kingdom of God!" (Mark 10:23). Mark records the reaction of the disciples. They are perplexed. All of their life they have been taught that there is an inseparable positive correlation between wealth and righteousness. If you are wealthy, God must have blessed you. Picking up on their befuddlement, Jesus drives a deeper wedge between righteousness and wealth with a graphic image: "It is easier for a camel to go through the eye of a needle than for someone who is rich to enter the kingdom of God" (Mark 10:25). Now the disciples are exasperated: "Then who can be saved?" (Mark 10:26).

Jesus allowed the disciples to live with conundrums. He intentionally set up mental train wrecks. Running on the same tracks toward each other were two diametrically opposed thoughts. No easy answers were provided, nor were there fill-in-the-blank workbooks. He wanted disciples who would have to think through the issues. Included in discipleship is the discipleship of the mind. Too much of the material that is produced under the heading of discipleship curriculum is spoon-fed pabulum. Jesus intentionally troubled the disciples by challenging their cherished assumptions.

In a discipling relationship, life circumstance becomes the setting for the exegetical work of God's Word. My discipling relationships over the years have offered no end of opportunities to reflect on the Word of God in the teachable moments. One of my discipling partners was in the midst of an interminable lawsuit over a dream house that had burned down during the latter stages of construction. Mike's first Sunday at our church was the Sunday following this upsetting experience. It "just so happened" that the Scripture and subject of that Sunday morning's message was Yahweh speaking to Moses via the burning bush. Mike immediately understood that the ashes of his home were his burning bush. Yet the event that grabbed his attention and brought him to the Lord continued through years of litigation to be the source of much further instruction. Assumed in our Americanized version of God's blessing is an ever-increasing financial position. Mike's financial position became ever decreasing following his coming to Christ. How do we understand God's blessing in these circumstances? We discussed how the American view of blessing had overshadowed Jesus' view.

The most crucial and climatic interactive dialogue between Jesus and the disciples centered on the personal question that every potential disciple of Jesus must answer. Jesus asked the disciples a sequence of two questions that moved from the general to the specific. His first question was a set-up: "Who do people say that I am?" (Mark 8:27). The disciples relayed the scuttlebutt that they had heard on the road. Then Jesus turned to them with *the* question, "But who do you say that I am?" (Mark 8:29). After Peter miraculously blurted out the right answer, "You are the Messiah," Jesus went on to fill out the conception of Messiah as a suffering servant in terms that were diametrically opposed to the popular conception. A dying messiah was unthinkable to Peter. In the space of a few moments Peter went from being an instrument of God's revelation to an unwitting tool of Satan. Peter rebuked Jesus for articulating the ridiculous idea that he would set his face to go to Jerusalem and die at the hands of unrighteous men. This notion of choosing to lay one's life down became the occasion for Jesus laying out the cost of discipleship for any who would follow him.

In addition to these interactive teaching moments, Jesus affirmed the disciples' value by including them as his assistants. On one occasion Jesus attempted to get away to a quiet place to debrief their mission foray. The crowds would not allow Jesus out of their sight so they followed him and the Twelve to a deserted place. Being far from a nearby town where the people could obtain food, the disciples became concerned that they had nothing to eat. Initially Jesus placed the responsibility upon the disciples to feed the five thousand. The disciples checked their treasury and determined that two hundred denarii would not go very far. At this point Jesus took over. He miraculously multiplied the five loaves and two fish that were available into enough food to feed the crowd. The disciples were prominent as Jesus' ushers at this outdoor gathering. They divided the crowds into groups of hundreds and fifties and distributed the bread and fish in an orderly fashion. The disciples in this instance were extensions of the ministry of Jesus to the crowds. They were visible and prominent, even as Jesus continued to be the one to whom the crowds looked.

There is a great training principle here. If we are to follow the model of Jesus, apprenticeship should be a part of all that we do so that ministry can be multiplied. Small-group leaders identify apprentices in their groups with the potential to lead. They are given increasing responsibility from week to week so that it is obvious to the other group members who are being groomed for future leadership. A pastor never visits the hospital or goes on a grief call alone, seeing it as the opportunity to train those who are called to caring ministry. When I was attempting to expand a seminar to help God's people discern their spiritual gifts and call to ministry, I rewrote the curriculum and taught it with two other lay leaders with teaching gifts. They put their fingerprints on the curriculum and their teaching style on the workshop. What we created and delivered together was by far better than anything I could have done on my own. When speaking opportunities arise, especially to teach in the areas of discipling or missions, I invite those with whom I have been in a discipling relationship, so that they can add their word of witness but also hear from me again the vision connected with these emphases.

A number of benefits accrue when assistants are publicly included in ministry. First, those assisting gain a sense of their value to the one who has included them. For the disciples, I am sure they began to realize their importance and value by the sheer public association with Jesus. Second, the public identification with a leader deepens their ownership of the mission. The mission of Jesus slowly became the disciples' mission through visibility. Third, apprenticeship heightens the learning curve. When one is being trained to lead a future mission, one's learning antenna is wired to observe more carefully and to seek answers to questions that will equip when one is in a position of responsibility.

In this second stage, where Jesus acted as the provocative teacher, he raised the bar for the disciples through his personalized instruction and pointed questioning, and through the lifting of their public profile.

DEVELOPMENTAL STAGE THREE:
JESUS, THE SUPPORTIVE COACH

In the third phase of Jesus' preparatory model, Jesus acts as the supportive coach by sending the Twelve and the seventy out on a short-term mission opportunity. From the time Jesus designated the Twelve to be apostles, he had this moment in mind. Their mission had been clearly defined. They were to be "sent out to proclaim the message, and to have authority to cast out demons" (Mark 3:14-15). Yet there was a time delay between Jesus' stated destination and the Twelve assuming this responsibility. Jesus wanted them to slowly live into this role. The sentence that best describes this stage is "You do, I help."

Jesus intentionally adjusts his leadership style again in order to move the disciples to a new stage of development. Jesus acts as the coach sending them on their mission and yet remains supportive, ready to debrief them upon their return. Jesus sends out the Twelve and the seventy into the fray with the knowledge that he will be there upon their return to cheer their successes and address their quandaries. While an apprentice probably never feels fully ready to assume the lead role, like baby birds Jesus' disciples needed to be pushed out of the nest to see if they were going to fly. They also knew that the nest was still there for them to return to after their initial flight.

Jesus was a model delegator. Once Jesus completed his instructions, the disciples not only knew their mission but also had specific guidelines to follow in order to accomplish it.

Matthew gives us the most detailed account of the mission on which Jesus sends the Twelve.

Clear instructions. Matthew introduces the mission with this line: "These twelve Jesus sent out with the following instructions" (Matthew 10:5). I often hear pastors say that they delegate ministry to members of their congregation, meaning that they have dumped a responsibility in the lap of a willing recipient without any clarity of mission or guidelines as to how to carry it out. Not so with Jesus. Note the specificity of Jesus' instructions (Matthew 10:5-15). The parameters of the mission were that they went only to the lost sheep of Israel, and not to the Gentiles. The focus of the mission was proclaiming the message of the kingdom. The demonstration of the mission was to cure the sick, raise the dead, cleanse the lepers and cast out demons. The means to accomplish the mission was that they were not to rely on any earthly means of support. They were to stay with those who received the message. The response to the mission was that if people did not welcome them, they were to walk away and leave the judgment to God.

Clear authority. To be effective, authority must be delegated along with responsibility to accomplish a mission. This again is where church management often gets cross-legged. In the church, people often feel that they have been given a responsibility without authority. Each decision must be approved by a higher up, because people have not been entrusted with the capacity to implement the direction they discern. Jesus gave the disciples the parameters in which to function and then gave them his full backing to accomplish what he gave them to do.

Clear expectations. After detailing the clear instructions and authority, Jesus also warned the disciples about what lay ahead (Matthew 10:16-42). He wove together the cost and privilege of discipleship. If popularity with the world was the disciples' hoped-for outcome, then they had the wrong cause. They would face a rough crowd. Jesus compared the world with a pack of wolves. Awaiting them would be floggings by the authorities and betrayal by family members. After all, if this is what happened to their master, how much more could the servants expect the same? And yet there is great privilege in representing the name of Jesus and bearing his fate. "Everyone therefore who acknowledges me before others, I also will acknowledge before my Father in heaven," Jesus says (Matthew 10:32). Just as a coach exhorts his players before a football game, "Leave it all on the field," so Jesus is saying, "Pay the necessary price, because you will have my approval."

The Twelve and the seventy engaged in this short-term mission project with the full knowledge that Jesus would be there for the debriefing upon their return. In a sense this was an experimental, limited foray that served as a precursor to the life mission that was ahead after Jesus returned to the Father. The Gospels convey a sense of excitement and questioning when the Twelve and the seventy reported back to Jesus. Mark captures their enthusiasm in this way: "The apostles gathered around Jesus, and told him all that they had done and taught" (Mark 6:30). Luke reports that the seventy "returned with joy" (Luke 10:17). Yet there were cases that appeared to be beyond their resources that demanded further instruction from Jesus.

What were the benefits for the disciples from the short-term mission? First, they gained confidence in the authority of Jesus. Just as Jesus promised, people were healed, demons were cast out, and the good news of the gospel was received. Jesus truly had given them his authority to carry out the mission! Second, they grew in competence. You can ultimately learn and develop only by doing. Toward the end of my first professional ministry with college students, one of our student leaders gave me what I took to be a backhanded compliment. She said, "You have really grown as a teacher." I should have said "Thank you" and left it at that. But my reply caused her to say, "When you first began teaching, you weren't very good." Ouch, but true. It was only through the students' patience and forbearance that my teaching gift emerged. Just so, the disciples needed a controled laboratory in which to practice.

But third, the disciples also faced their shortcomings. It is when we get in over our heads, beyond our confidence and competence, that we are truly open to learning. An exasperated father approached Jesus because his disciples could not cast out a demon that tormented his son. Jesus proceeded with considerable impatience to do what the disciples could not. Later the disciples took advantage of the private moment to ask Jesus, "Why could we not cast it out?" (Mark 9:28). Jesus says essentially that this kind of an entrenched demonic spirit requires another level of prayer and fasting.

Delegation is a necessary stage to faith and leadership development. When a child learns to ride a bike, at some point the training wheels have to come off. The maiden voyage is a combination of terror and thrill. We make our way in wobbly fashion down the sidewalk and hope our crash is softened by the neighbor's lawn. We pick ourselves up and get back on the bike and try again and again. Eventually riding a bike becomes an internalized behavior so that no matter how long the time gaps between rides, we know how to keep our balance. Growth in serving Jesus is always like that. We must go where we have never gone before, with all the terror and thrill that comes with new territory. We find that Jesus is there to support and do through us just what he said he would. Jesus is never more pleased than when we trust him.

DEVELOPMENTAL STAGE FOUR:
JESUS, THE ULTIMATE DELEGATOR

Jesus staked his entire ministry on the preparation of the Twelve to carry on his mission after he returned to the Father. The time had come to send the disciples on their mission of reproduction. Jesus had a divine appointment with the cross, which the Scripture refers to as "the hour" (Mark 14:41; John 4:21; 12:23; 16:25; 17:1) or "his hour" (John 7:30; 8:20; 13:1). "The hour has come" converges with the transference of Jesus' ministry to the Twelve. Jesus' mission is complete in his death and resurrection. And at this time Jesus makes it clear that the focus of his work has been preparing the disciples to assume their leadership role under the guidance of his Spirit, not his physical presence. This stage is described by the sentence "You do, I watch."

Jesus' precrucifixion ministry concludes by his huddling with the Twelve around the Passover meal (John 13—17). The foundational importance of the Twelve to his ongoing mission is demonstrated by sharing his last hours alone with them. We come to a most sacred moment. We are allowed to eavesdrop on Jesus' final prayer before his rendezvous with death. What was on Jesus' heart? Two things: Jesus anticipated a reunion with his Father, and he prayed exclusively for the Twelve.

Jesus is fully conscious that he is completing what the Father had sent him to do. "I glorified you on earth by finishing the work that you gave me to do" (John 17:4). He nostalgically longs to return to his privileged position of a face-to-face relationship with the Father, which had been true prior to the creation of the world. Jesus is homesick. "So now, Father, glorify me in your own presence with the glory that I had in your presence before the world existed" (John 17:5). Jesus recalls life at home in the heart of the Father. He can't wait to salve the ache of separation that will be complete in face-to-face communion.

Though this prayer is wrapped in an atmosphere of Jesus' longing to be at home, the center of the prayer focuses solely on the Twelve. Jesus says that he doesn't even pray on behalf of the lost and rebellious world, but for those that the Father has given him out of the world (John 17:9). The final preparation of the Twelve was a significant part of finishing his work. His work would not have been completed until the Twelve were ready to assume their foreordained position. The tragedy is that most Christian leaders have placed almost no priority on transitional leadership. It is generally fair to say that the effectiveness of one's ministry is to be measured by how well it flourishes after one's departure.

For what does Jesus pray for his disciples? He prays for their protection (John 17:11); that they may be one (John 17:11); that they would be kept from the evil one; that they would not fall into apostasy, as did Judas; that Jesus' joy would be complete in them (John 17:13); that they would be made holy in the truth of God's Word. Then he makes the transitional mission statement: "As you have sent me into the world, so I have sent them into the world" (John 17:18). His ministry has now become their ministry. Not only are they sent, but also they are to reproduce. Jesus prays not only for these Twelve but also for those who would believe because of their witness (John 17:20). Earlier in this Passover gathering, Jesus said, "My Father is glorified by this, that you bear much fruit and become my disciples" (John 15:8). In John's typical fashion, the nature of the fruit bearing is deliciously ambiguous. We should take this quantitatively, that more disciples are made, and qualitatively, that the disciples would reflect the character and life of Jesus. As Dawson Trotman said, the apostles are "born to reproduce," which can be said of every disciple of Jesus.

Here is the challenge to all pastors and Christian leaders. Where are the men and women in whom we are multiplying ourselves so that the ministry carries on long after we have gone? How would your ministry be different if you placed the highest priority on selecting, motivating and training lay leaders that could carry on as much as possible the mission of the parish after you were gone? Take a moment to evaluate how your ministry would be different if you made a few the priority, as Jesus did. What if you adopted Jesus' model of training a few by guiding them through all these developmental stages to the point where their ministry was not reliant upon you? How would the way you spend your time change? How would this affect your weekly schedule? What would you have to give up doing in order to train people? What skills would you have to acquire that are not currently a part of your repertoire? Robert Coleman writes, "What really counts in the ultimate perpetuation of our work is the faithfulness with which our converts go out and make leaders out of their converts, not simply more followers."[15]

Jesus employed an empowerment model of servant leadership and training. Whereas pastors and ministry leaders today tend to be satisfied in having people become dependent upon their teaching and care, Jesus wanted self-initiating, reproducing, fully devoted followers. Today's pastor often looks at the church as the context in which he or she can minister while gathering a congregation as the audience. Jesus, by contrast, thought that multiplication of ministry in a chosen few was the measurement of success. I am sorry to say that what Coleman prophetically wrote in 1963 is still largely true: "Jesus' plan has not been disavowed; it has been ignored."[16] If we want to see self-initiating, reproducing, fully devoted followers be the mark of our ministry, we must adopt Jesus' method of investing in a few as the foundation upon which to build our ministry.

In chapter five we will see that the apostle Paul had an empowerment similar to Jesus', though he used different images to convey the same reality.

5

PAUL'S EMPOWERMENT MODEL
Spiritual Parenting

In chapter four we examined Jesus' preparatory disciple-making model with insights from *Situational Leadership*. My thesis is that Jesus adapted his leadership style to the readiness level of the disciples. His goal was that the Twelve would continue his mission. The incarnate Son of God intended from the beginning to extend his life and ministry through this small core of disciples and, through them, set up an interlocking, multigenerational chain of disciple making (John 17:20).

We turn our attention now to the apostle Paul's model of disciple making. We must first note that the language that runs throughout the Gospels and the book of Acts is absent in Paul's nomenclature. Whereas the terms "make disciples" and "be a disciple" dominate Jesus' vocabulary and the historical accounts of the early church, they are nowhere to be found in Paul's letters. In fact, Paul never speaks of having disciples![1] His efforts were directed toward helping the church understand that Christians are about being "in Christ" or "Christ in you." This does not mean that the concept of discipleship is absent in Paul's thought. Being a self-initiating, reproducing, fully devoted follower of Christ is as much present in Paul's thought as it is in Jesus' thought. It is just stated in different terms.

The defining, though not exclusive, metaphor that shapes Paul's understanding of the goal and the process of disciple making is spiritual parenting. Paul's writings are sprinkled with images of spiritual fatherhood and motherhood: addressing those under his care as infants and children; characterizing himself as a nursing mother, or as a mother in the agony of labor; stating that the goal in Christ is to grow up to maturity (adulthood). Though Paul does not restrict himself to this group of family images, the lens that shapes the primary way he views the process and product of being in Christ is parental.

THE GOAL OF PARENTING

In a healthy family, the goal of parents is to grow children into independent, responsible and caring adults. Jack and Judy Balswick provide an excellent overview of family images in the growth process.

> The Christian life is described in various New Testament passages as growth from spiritual infancy to maturity. The new believer starts as an infant and eventually grows up in Christ. One moves from a state of dependency, in which others model, teach, and disciple, to a mature walk with God. As this growth occurs, the believer also begins to assume discipling responsibility for others. While it is true that the believer is always dependent on God and the Holy Spirit in that growth process, there is a natural progression in maturity which leads the believer to be used by God to serve and minister to others.[2]

The Balswicks quite naturally weave together a biblical conception of parenting with the parental images for the Christian growth process. "Parenting which empowers children to maturity is conceptually similar to the New Testament depiction of discipling."[3]

The way the Balswicks conceive of the goal of Christian parenting sounds much like a definition of Christian maturity. "Successful parenting will result in the children's gaining as much personal power as the parents themselves have. In the Christian context, children who have been empowered love God and their neighbors as themselves. They are capable of going beyond themselves to reach out to others."[4]

It should not surprise us that the goal of Christian parenting is identical to the goal of discipling. The primary discipleship unit is the Christian home. The primary disciplers are parents. That Paul should weave parental and developmental images into his understanding of the maturity process makes all the sense in the world.

PAUL'S EMPOWERMENT GOAL

It is in vogue for churches to write mission statements. In the church I served most recently as senior pastor, it felt like it took longer to write a mission statement than it did to write the final version of the United States Constitution. Over a three-year period we deforested much of Northern California with our discarded drafts. I look back on that effort with some embarrassment, because only in retrospect has it dawned on me that Jesus had already provided the mission statement for every church. It is popularly called the Great Commission (Matthew 28:18-20). Instead of coming up with a new mission, as if it must be unique for each church, we should redirect our energy to making a fresh statement of Jesus' original marching orders. For example, Willow Creek Community Church has the most often quoted rewrite of Jesus' words as its stated mission: "To turn irreligious people into fully devoted followers of Christ."

For Paul the primary goal of the Christian life is to reach the state of maturity in Christ. The apostle Paul personalized Jesus' clarion call in writing his own mission statement. If you listen carefully to Colossians 1:28-29, you will hear the echo of Jesus' command to "go and make disciples." Paul articulates the call upon his life: "It is he [Jesus] whom we proclaim, warning everyone and teaching everyone in all wisdom, so that we may present everyone mature in Christ. For this I toil and struggle with all the energy that he powerfully inspires within me." One purpose demands all of Paul's effort and energy—to bring everyone to maturity in Christ. One way to discern a personal call of God is to be attentive to what gives you energy. In Colossians 1:29 Paul tells us that he puts his energy into bringing people to adulthood in Christ. Paul begins, "For this I toil." The root of the Greek word for "toil" means beatings or the weariness that comes from being struck. As this term evolved, it became an analogy for the weariness that comes from hard work, labor or striving.

This image is coupled with "struggle." "For this I toil and struggle." A literal transliteration from the Greek would be "agonize." On another occasion Paul used this same word to compare the Christian life with that of an athlete: "Athletes exercise [agonize] self-control in all things; they do it to receive a perishable wreath, but we an imperishable one" (1 Corinthians 9:25). In articulating his personal mission statement, Paul says that his singular focus is to assist everyone he encounters toward maturity in Christ.

The root of the word for "maturity" in Greek is *telos,* which means "end" or "goal." Viewing maturity as the goal of the Christian life is a further indication that Paul views the discipleship process in terms of parental empowerment. To be mature is to be fully adult. J. B. Lightfoot believes that Paul has intentionally imported this word from the ancient mystery religions. According to the mystery religions, the fully instructed were the mature, as opposed to novices. In the early church the baptized were the *teleios* ("mature" or "complete"), as opposed to the catechumens, who were still in a preparatory or instructional period prior to baptism. To further underscore the family connections with this word, Paul contrasts being mature with being infants or children in the faith. Paul chides the Corinthians "as infants in Christ," who are still drinking milk when they should be eating solid food (1 Corinthians 3:1-2). Later in this same letter, Paul draws a direct contrast between being children versus being adults: "Brothers and sisters, do not be children in your thinking; rather, be infants in evil, but in thinking be adults [*teleios*]" (1 Corinthians 14:20). In Ephesians Paul states that the mature (*teleios*) have grown to the measure of full stature of Christ, whereas those who are children in the faith are unstable, tossed around and carried away by the wind of every new doctrine that sounds enticing (Ephesians 4:13-14).

As I stated, though the familial or parental images dominate and shape Paul's conception of discipleship, these are not the only images. Maturity is the end product that Paul is attempting to produce, but the word tells us little about the process of how to get there. Paul fleshes out what he means by maturity by saying that the purpose of existence is to be "conformed to the image of [God's] Son" (Romans 8:29).

TRANSFORMATION: PRODUCT AND PROCESS

Transformation captures the product and the process of Christian discipleship. The Greek root here is *morphoō*, which has slipped into pop vocabulary as "morphing." Morphing is associated with computer-generated images. We watch the transformation as the features of a woman's face morph into those of a man, or the like. Computers allow us to instantaneously morph into new bodies that look twenty pounds lighter or enable us to see how we might look wearing a tuxedo or a formal gown or lying on a Hawaiian beach in our swimsuit.

Morphing implies that where we are and where we want to be are two different things. We are reclamation projects. During my growing up years I watched a dramatic transformation take place. Scholl Canyon in Southern California was a gorge where the trash trucks unloaded their rotting garbage and human discards. Yet in my twenties I had the opportunity to play golf on this same site. It had been morphed from a stinking landfill into a beautifully manicured, green playground overlooking the San Fernando Valley in Southern California. Once the ravine was filled to capacity, it was transformed from a refuse depository into a new creation, or should I say a place of re-creation.

Morphē in the original Greek means "the inward and real formation of the essential nature of a person or living being." This is contrasted with another word, *schēma*, also translated "form." Whereas *schēma* deals with the outward, changeable form, *morphē* is about a new, unchangeable core. *Schēma* has to do with outwardly blending in, like a chameleon adapting to the flora and fauna. Paul contrasts *schēma* and *morphē* when he exhorts the Romans, "Do not be conformed *[syschēmatizomai]* to this world, but be transformed *[metamorphoomai]* by the renewal of your mind" (Romans 12:2 RSV). Paul understands transformation as an inside job, whereas conformity is adapting outwardly to the circumstance. One translator captures Paul's use of "conformity" this way: "Do not adapt to the external and fleeting fashion of this world." *Metamorphoomai* ("metamorphosis") is the word used to describe the transformation of Jesus on the Mount of Transfiguration (Mark 9:2). For a moment Jesus appeared on the outside with the same dazzling glory that is true of his inward nature.

A paragraph ago I did not tell you the whole story about the transformation of Scholl Canyon from a landfill to a golf course. I played golf only once on that transformed course, for emanating from below the thin layer of topsoil was a nauseating stench. All I could think of when standing on the putting greens was that just below my feet was a bubbling chemical caldron. The landfill had been schematized, but it had not been morphed. A superficial change occurred, but there was no permanent transformation from within. A true transformation would have meant removal of the rubbish, to be replaced by clean soil. This is why Paul constantly connects transformation with the images of "putting off" the old nature and "putting on" the new nature (Ephesians 4:17-32).

For Paul, the fully devoted, reproducing disciple is one who has grown to reflect the character of Jesus in his or her life. The process of transformation removes all that reflects the old, sinful self, while the scent of Christ permeates the whole being from the inside out. Maturity for Paul is our readiness to have Jesus reflect his nature through every aspect of our being.

If this is the goal, then how did Paul go about helping people to grow toward maturity or Christlike transformation? This parental model can be broken into a series of roles that assist a believer to move from infancy to adulthood. The discipleship process parallels the way in which parents must adjust how they exercise their role to grow their children into responsible, caring, empowering adults.

LIFE STAGE	LIFE STAGE NEED	DISCIPLE'S ROLE	PAUL'S ROLE
Infancy	Modeling and direction	Imitation	Model
Childhood	Unconditional love and protection	Identification	Hero
Adolescence	Increased freedom and identity formation	Exhortation	Coach
Adulthood	Mutuality and reciprocity	Participation	Peer

Figure 5.1. Paul's parental empowerment model

DEVELOPMENTAL STAGE ONE: INFANCY (IMITATION)

Paul combines his parental self-understanding with a call to the Corinthians to imitate his life. He views his relationship to them as a father to his "beloved children." As father, he was instrumental in bringing about the spiritual birth of many of the Corinthians: "Indeed, in Christ Jesus I became your father through the gospel" (1 Corinthians 4:15). Then Paul draws out the natural implications: "I appeal to you, then, be imitators of me" (1 Corinthians 4:16). In Paul's day, fathers were expected to model appropriate behavior and be copied by their children. "Regard your father's conduct as the law and strive to imitate and emulate your father's virtue."[5]

The word imitate here is *mimeomai*, from which we get the English word *mimic*. *Mimeomai* is used in a number of places (1 Corinthians 11:1; Philippians 3:17; 1 Thessalonians 1:6-7; 2 Thessalonians 3:7, 9), accompanied often by the word *typos*, which is translated variously as "example," "model" or "pattern." In 1 Corinthians 11:1 Paul qualifies his previously unqualified admonition to imitate himself by adding, "Be imitators of me, as I am of Christ." In other words, his converts were to imitate the evidence of Christ in him. Why does Paul not simply say, "Imitate Christ"? Why does he place himself between Christ and the Corinthians? When I first read these exhortations to self-imitation, my thoughts were, *Paul, how can you say such a thing? You arrogant so and so, how conceited can you be?* It was only as my understanding of the way God works developed that I realized that Paul was espousing good incarnational theology. God embodies his presence. He came to us fully in Jesus. Then he placed his life in his followers, who become reflections of him. This is the way God has chosen to work—putting up life next to life.

Imitation has the sense of following the lifestyle of another. Paul says to the Philippians, "Brothers and sisters, join in imitating [*mimeomai*] me, and observe those who live according to the example [*typos*] you have in us" (Philippians 3:17). He adds that he, along with his coauthor Timothy, serve as their models (*typos*). *Typos* is derived from the word meaning "to strike," or the mark of a blow or the impression left. A hammer blow on a piece of wood leaves an indentation. A signet ring pressed against hot wax leaves the impression of a seal. In other words, Paul's and Timothy's lifestyles provide the mold for the Philippians. These same two words are coupled in 1 Thessalonians 1:6-7 and 2 Thessalonians 3:7, 9.

Now what was it that Paul expected these churches would imitate? Was he seeking plastic replicas of himself? Was he expecting that everyone have his go-for-broke, single-minded personality? Maybe he expected everyone to get on the road and suffer as an apostle? Was it his combative style that Paul was urging that they would follow? This is an important question, since some disciple-making emphases seem to demand superficial replication of the habits and mannerism of a dominant personality. A generation ago I could easily tell the followers of a particular disciple maker because they kept three-by-five cards in their pockets. They were taught that a disciple was a ready learner and must have the capacity to capture an insight or quotable quote in a moment's notice. This is mild compared with the cultlike characteristics of extreme hierarchical models. Some have promoted a chain-of-command approach that says that the one being discipled must have all decisions ratified by the discipler because the discipler is the voice of God to them. Is this what Paul had in mind when he said, "Imitate me"?

We don't need to speculate about what Paul meant when he called people to imitate him as he imitated Christ. Paul gave a clear description of what he thought was worth emulating when he met with the Ephesian elders in Miletus (Acts 20:17-38). When Paul arrived at the port city of Miletus during his second missionary journey, he sent for the elders of the Ephesian church to offer one last word of encouragement. Prior to their wrenching goodbye, Paul reminded them of his model while he was with them. What did he emphasize? His life was one of humility and tears, enduring the hardship of the plots of Jews that dogged this former Pharisee wherever he went. He remained focused on the core message of the gospel, not compromising its call to repentance, whether that was in public or from house to house. His sole concern was that he might complete the work that Jesus had assigned. So what does Paul want them to imitate? I think Paul might summarize what he would have us imitate like this: "Just as I am willing to die to myself, so that Christ might fully shine through me, do so yourself. I am fulfilling the assignment Christ has given me; you do so as well. Be all that you are to be in Christ."

When Paul calls for Christ be formed in us, he wants us to be the best us that God designed us to be. C. S. Lewis has addressed this issue powerfully. We might think that we are to relinquish our lives to Christ and then Jesus blots out our unique personality in order to make us all alike in him. Lewis reminds us that the opposite is true.

> The more we get what we now call "ourselves" out of the way and let Him take us over, the more truly ourselves we become. There is so much of Him that millions and millions of "little Christs," all different, will still be too few to express Him fully. He made them all. He invented—as an author invents characters in a novel—all the different [people] that you and I were intended to be. In that sense our real selves are all waiting for us in Him. It is no good trying to "be myself" without Him. The more I resist Him and try to live on my own, the more I become dominated by my own heredity and upbringing and surroundings and natural desires. . . . It is when I turn to Christ, when I give myself up to His Personality, that I first begin to have a real personality of my own.[6]

As a discipler, Paul believed that something about the way he lived his life in Christ was worth being caught and modeled by others. This is a necessary element in our ability to invest in others as well.

DEVELOPMENTAL STAGE TWO:
IDENTIFICATION (CHILDHOOD)

Loving parents tie their welfare and happiness to the welfare and happiness of their children. In this regard Paul had the heart of a parent when it came to the welfare of his spiritual children. Paul's ability to enter into the lives of his converts allowed them to turn around and fully identify with him. In chapter three I described the impact that Don had on my life during my impressionable college years. I was soft clay in search of someone to help shape my life purpose. I desired to be like Don because I identified with him. Yet I identified with him because he gave himself to me. When I recall times with Don, I see in my mind's eye engaging conversations seated side by side on a bench next to a tennis court or across from each other at a picnic table in a park. What I remember from those times is being allowed into the heart of this man. He shared not only his love for Jesus but also those tender and tough places where Jesus needed to remove the dross of his life. The passion I observed in Don made me want to be like him.

Imitation becomes motivating through identification. "Identification is the process in which a person believes himself to be like another person in some respects, experiences the successes and defeats as his own, and consciously or unconsciously models his behavior after him. . . . The fact that there is emotional involvement with the other person distinguishes identification from mere imitation."[7]

Emotional identification is engendered in the discipleship relationship by the discipler making a life investment. Paul identified with and entered fully into the lives of those he served. Paul used maternal and paternal images to convey the connection of his life with their welfare.

Paul boldly embraced feminine images to convey his emotional connection with those he longed to bring into Christian adulthood. Perhaps the most unusual use of the maternal image is when Paul refers to the Galatians as "my little children, for whom I am again in the pain of childbirth until Christ is formed in you" (Galatians 4:19). As a male, I don't know what Paul knew about labor pains. He most likely had heard the wailing of women in labor and thought this agony was analogous to his feelings about the Galatians. On the long night in which our daughter was born, my usually immaculately kept wife had no concern about her appearance. Her sweat-soaked brow had straightened out the curls on her forehead. Her body buckled into a V-shape every five minutes. I have long since tried to forget the sounds that ejaculated from deep down. Then came the pronouncement of the early morning, "This is the worst night of my life!" Just so, Paul had tied his welfare to Christ being formed in the Galatians.

When we turn to Paul's first letter to the Thessalonians, he continues the maternal image when he says, "We were gentle among you, like a nurse tenderly caring for her own children." (1 Thessalonians 2:7). A good case can be made that "nurse" here is "nursing mother," which makes sense when coupled with "caring for her own children." There is nothing like the understanding of a mother's love. The low point of my adolescent development came in the transition from elementary school to junior high. I lived in a constant state of fear of failure in the classroom, fear of loss of friendships and fear of not performing athletically. My world was not a safe place. Many a night I would sob myself to sleep. Watching a son go through this broke the heart of my mother. She could not stand to see her child in pain. I have warm recollections of bedside talks and soothing poems meant to bring comfort to my troubled soul. So Paul was to the Thessalonians. Paul draws on the image of Moses taking up the people of Israel into his bosom "as a nurse takes up a suckling child." This is the gentle side of Paul that is not our usual image.

Eugene Peterson captures this section well in The Message: "We were never patronizing, never condescending, but we cared for you the way a mother cares for her children. We loved you dearly. Not just content to pass on the Message, we wanted to give you our hearts. And we did" (1 Thessalonians 2:8). It was not a matter of dropping gospel bombs and then moving on to the next town.

Churches often invite in a guest speaker who comes to give a pre-packaged message, but one does not get the sense that such guest speakers have come to give themselves. As a pastor I had a dream of a biannual teacher or prophet-in-residence who would come for a month and live among us. The hope was not only to get their impassioned message but also to live with their heart. I wanted more than the in-and-out speaker. The dream died because numerous invitations yielded only one person willing to make such a commitment. Paul came and stayed. He gave himself, not just his message. He could not conceive of the message apart from it being incarnated through his being.

Paul balances his maternal self-description within a few verses by adding, "As you know, we dealt with each one of you like a father with his children, urging and encouraging you and pleading that you lead a life worthy of God, who calls you into his own kingdom and glory" (1 Thessalonians 2:11-12). Wise parents know to treat each one of their children as individuals. What motivates one child may be demotivating for another. Whereas an agreeable temperament may be characteristic of one child, another may be constantly pressing the boundaries. One child may have an artistic bent, whereas another has the genetic code of an accountant. Paul says that he dealt with "each one of you like a father." Discipling is about respecting the individuality of a disciple and assisting his or her uniqueness to blossom in accord with God's design. In the developmental process a watchful parent can already see in the childhood years the particular inclination of each child.

Paul selects three verbs to describe the nature of his fatherly discipling relationship with the Thessalonians. Each of these words conveys a different strategy of motivation that depends upon the individual state of growth and disposition. "We dealt with each of you like a father with his children, urging . . . encouraging . . . pleading."

Parakaleō is the same descriptor that Jesus gives to the Holy

Spirit when he says, "I will send you another counselor, advocate, helper, encourager." No one English word is adequate to capture the various nuances of the term. Literally the word means "to come alongside to help." Paul came alongside, urging them, sometimes bringing comfort, at other times acting as their cheerleader and still other times exhorting them to live up to their calling.

Coupled with urging, encouraging (*paramytheomai*) probably means to be encouraged to continue in the course they are on. It carries the sense of "to build up, or to give a reason for hope." The Christian life can be discouraging when we battle our inner demons and the hostile world. We need hope to carry on.

The root of "pleading" (*martyreō*) here is "witness" or "martyr." The word could just as easily have been translated "charging." As a coach might give the impassioned speech to fire up his or her players, so there are appropriate times for disciplers to call the best out of those in whom they are investing. Paul needed to say on occasion, "Get out of your comfort zone and take some risk in service to Jesus."

Paul did not guard himself against disappointment. He made himself fully vulnerable to the despair that comes when a disciple disappoints. Love requires identification, not self-protection. At the childhood stage of growth, disciples need to know that their welfare is another's deepest concern.

DEVELOPMENTAL STAGE THREE: EXHORTATION (ADOLESCENCE)

The adolescent stage of discipleship is very much like the adolescent stage of children. During adolescence a critical issue is building confidence so that teenagers can blossom into their own persons. This occurs by allowing teens to learn by trial and error. Parents limit the amount of rescuing, while offering support and consolation as needed. In other words, adolescents grow up by facing the consequences of their actions.

The image of a coach is an appropriate one for this stage. The coach is in the privileged position of helping people to see the potential they didn't know was there. Tom Landry, the legendary coach of the Dallas Cowboys, defined coaching as "making men do what they don't want, so that they can become what they want to be."[8] Elton Trueblood proposed the image of "player-coach" as the best modern metaphor for the equipping pastor. "The glory of the coach is that of being the discoverer, the developer, and the trainer of the powers of other men. This is exactly what we mean when we use the Biblical terminology about the equipping ministry."[9]

In 2 Timothy, generally considered Paul's last known correspondence, he melds the image of coach and father. Paul conveys in this final letter that the end of his ministry is imminent: "The time of my departure has come" (2 Timothy 4:6). Paul's agenda is to ensure the transmission of the gospel to the next generation. What the Lord has allotted him to do is complete. So he is thinking about effecting the transition to those that have been in the battle with him. Paul's leg of the race is almost over. But before he receives his reward, he must pass the baton.

One of the persons to carry on in his absence is his beloved son in the faith, Timothy. You get the sense that there were few people in Paul's life who held the place of affection as did Timothy. True, Paul was Timothy's spiritual father, but my guess is if Paul had the choice of a biological son, it would have been Timothy. "To Timothy, my beloved child," he begins this letter. In his first letter to Timothy he addresses him as "my loyal child." To the Corinthians Paul wrote that he was sending them Timothy, "who is my beloved and faithful child in the Lord" (1 Corinthians 4:17).

It is the natural order of things that faith is passed from parent to child. Every son or daughter longs to receive the blessing of his or her father. About a month after my father's death in 1994, I went on a two-day silent retreat, seeking some space to process my emotions in the aftermath of my parents' deaths, which occurred within a month of each other. I found myself drawn to

Paul's second letter to Timothy. All of my life I had wanted my father to be in the position to offer his blessing and exhortation to carry on the faith. Now I knew with finality that day would never come. There was a sense that I had missed out on the natural order of things.

Oh, how I envy Timothy. Paul is the coach/father exhorting Timothy to live up to his calling. Paul gets to the core of his intent when he says to his son, "Carry out your ministry fully" (2 Timothy 4:5). Paul follows up that plea immediately with his own example: "I have fought the good fight, I have finished the race, I have kept the faith" (2 Timothy 4:7). Paul's message to Timothy is, You do the same! As I see it, 2 Timothy is a motivational letter. If you were to read this letter from one angle only, listing the different techniques Paul uses to motivate Timothy, you would not miss much of the content. All of this variety of motivational means is designed to say one thing to Timothy in the adolescent stage of development: Become the person God has designed you to be.

It is human nature to move toward comfort and avoid pain. We want to live a quiet and peaceable life and to be left alone and insulated from other people's problems. Our sense of urgency dissipates, and we fail to remain on high alert. We lose our focus, and our aims become fuzzy. We need settings where the coach can get in our face. All too often I have watched myself and others slowly turn down the temperature to where we become lukewarm and insipid. We need purifying and refining contexts where the best is continuously called out of us. Humans follow the law of entropy; we wind down, and our energy dissipates unless the poker stokes the coals of our lives and stirs them up again.

DEVELOPMENTAL STAGE FOUR: PARTICIPATION (ADULTHOOD)

The goal of the discipling process is to arrive at maturity. The Balswicks state the goal of parenting this way: "God's ideal is that children mature to the point where they and their parents empower each other."[10] Mutuality marks the stage of maturity. Parents get to the point where they can learn from their children. "Reciprocal giving and receiving is an indication of a mature relationship [between parents and children]."[11] As parents, my wife and I are at the enjoyable stage of relating to our recently married daughter, who has charted her life direction in medicine. She enjoys instructing her aging baby-boom parents in things medical. We consult with her about our aches and pains. We laugh together at our constantly falling for the promises of various anti-aging products that play on our fears of getting older. She has incorporated our values into her life trajectory. We have come to the point of letting go and become much more adult partners with our daughter and son-in-law.

Mutuality and partnership marked the adult stage of Paul's ministry. In the early stages of infancy and childhood development in the faith, the discipler is much more directive. Imitation and identification are about investing and serving as an illustration of the way things are to be. Once we move to the adolescent stage of growth, it is marked by exhorting the person to become all that God intended him or her to be. An increasing amount of freedom and experimentation is permitted. At the adult stage, the learning becomes a mutual process of upbuilding. Paul treats the Romans as adults when he writes, "For I am longing to see you so that I may share with you some spiritual gift to strengthen you—or rather so that we may be mutually encouraged by each other's faith, both yours and mine" (Romans 1:11-12). Paul dignified the Romans by saying that he was not coming just to give to them but to receive from them as well. Healthy relationships are mutual. This does not imply that maturity levels are equal. But it does say that no matter one's maturity level in Christ, there is something to offer as well as receive. Paul, no matter his stature in the faith, would never outgrow the need to receive the benefit of some spiritual gift the Romans could offer.

In his ministry, Paul viewed himself as a partner and colaborer with others in the gospel. We have a significant list of names of people with whom Paul shared in mutual labor in the gospel: Timothy, Titus, Epaphroditus, Silvanus, Priscilla, Aquila, Euodia, Synteche, Onesiphorus (and see Romans 16). Though in terms of authority Paul was an apostle, he restrains himself from a heavy-handed use of that authority. For example, he writes to Philemon about his runaway slave, Onesimus. He addresses Philemon in this salutation as a "dear friend and co-worker" (Philemon 2). Urging Philemon to receive back his slave, Onesimus, Paul says that as an apostle he could exercise that authority in the form of a command, but instead, out of respect for Philemon, he appeals on the basis of love.

Paul avoids hierarchical language in relationship to those who share with him in the ministry of the gospel. Missional relationships are collegial. In 2 Corinthians 8:23 he refers to Titus as "my partner and co-worker in your service." The term *partner* derives from the familiar *koinōnia,* meaning that which we share in common, often translated as "fellowship." "We are in this together" is Paul's message. Paul identifies Epaphroditus as "my brother and co-worker and fellow soldier" (Philippians 2:25). Later in this same letter, Paul is concerned about unity between two women, Euodia and Syntyche. He says of them that they "struggled beside me in the work of the gospel, together with Clement and the rest of my co-workers" (Philippians 4:2-3). Though Paul is not shy about calling those who are stuck in infancy to grow up, he does not stress the hierarchical nature of the discipling process. And though there are differences among us in maturity level, stressing these differences or defining relationships based upon them is not helpful.

Paul's parental discipling model always had the goal of encouraging people to become all they were intended to be in Christ. Paul's desire was for completeness in each believer, meaning fulfilling a person's unique, God-given design. Making people replicas of himself was not on Paul's agenda. He did not see himself as the sage on the stage but the guide on the side. Paul had a mission model of discipleship that conveyed that we are in partnership together to take the gospel to those who desperately need to hear of the love of God. When mission predominates, partnership and mutuality mark the relationship between a leader and God's people.

Paul's parental discipling model was layered. On the foundation of imitation came identification marking the infancy and childhood stages of faith. As disciples began to develop into their identity, an exhortation to grow up into their potential marked Paul's communication. Then finally Paul expected people to grow to maturity by entering into full participation with him in the mission of the gospel.

SUMMARY OF THE MODEL OF JESUS AND PAUL

This chapter concludes our reflections on the biblical vision of disciple making. We noticed that Jesus intentionally called a few because that was the only way to internalize his message and mission and to multiply himself. His intent was that his ministry would become the ministry of the Twelve and be the means by which he extended himself to the world. To prepare the Twelve, Jesus followed a *Situational Leadership* model, adjusting his leadership style to the readiness of his followers. As Jesus adjusted his leadership to match the readiness of the disciples, he also changed styles to provoke them to the next level of growth. Jesus shifted his roles from living example, to provocative teacher, to supportive coach, and finally to ultimate delegator. Though Paul's language and images differed, his goal and process mirrored the model of his Lord.

We come to the "now what" section of our reflection. How do we take this biblical vision and translate it into a church-based model of disciple making? This is the point where we have usually failed. Many of us have a working knowledge of what I have covered in these last three chapters, but we need to take the biblical imperative and put it into a workable scheme. This is the connection that the next chapters will make for you.

PART THREE

Multiplying Reproducing Discipleship Groups

Church-Based Strategy for Disciple Making

6

LIFE INVESTMENT
It's All About Relationships

We have come to the hinge in our examination of how people grow into self-initiating, reproducing, fully devoted disciples of Jesus. Hinges are small connectors. Without a hinge, a door cannot swing freely in its frame and therefore fulfill its purpose. So often the church is like a detached door leaning up against, but not connected to the biblical frame. The Scriptures provide not only the message but also the method for growing God's people to maturity. Yet we do not connect Jesus' and Paul's models for growing mature believers to a workable, practical process of making disciples.

Given Jesus' and Paul's models of disciple making, what principles can we extract that provide the connectors to a contemporary, church-based strategy of making reproducing disciples of Jesus? In this and the next two chapters we will explore three foundational principles upon which to build a process that leads to an intergenerational multiplication of fully devoted followers of Christ. The first hinge is life investment, or how we shift from an emphasis on making disciples through programs to making disciples through relationships (chap. 6). The second hinge is multiplication through the generations, or how we can disciple people to maturity but also to reproduction (chap. 7). The third hinge is transformation, which involves the necessary relational conditions to create a continuous process of transformation into Christlikeness and the impetus to carry on an ever-expanding discipling network (chap. 8).

DISCIPLES ARE MADE THROUGH LIFE INVESTMENT

Disciple making is not a six-week, ten-week or even a thirty-week program. Adding components that make a program more rigorous or time-consuming to call forth the truly committed does not produce disciples. Programs tend to be information- or knowledge-based, focus on one preparing for the many, require regimentation or synchronization and foster an atmosphere of low personal accountability (see chap. 2).

What is the usual approach to disciple making within the church or ministry today? The following scenario is far too often repeated. Frustration rises within the professional staff and governing board after repeated attempts have been made to recruit people to fill ministry positions. These conscription efforts are met with resistance or the realization that there is a limited pool of qualified people. The symptom of empty ministry positions leads to the diagnosis that there is a disciple-making deficit. With a clear eye on the problem we conclude that we don't have qualified ministry volunteers because we have not been intentional about growing self-initiating, reproducing disciples of Jesus. The solution is to call a committee whose task it is to come up with a discipleship program. Frank Tillapaugh asks sarcastically, "What is a committee? A committee is a group of people who get together to answer two questions: What should we do? and Who can we get to do it?"[1]

The committee scours the landscape for a discipleship program that has had proven success. This usually means that they are looking for a system and a curriculum that can be easily implemented in order to provide an accelerated solution to the ministry recruitment problem. The program is located. The prepackaged curriculum is accepted as is or adapted to the particular ministry, and then it is implemented. With great fanfare and high expectations the new program is announced as the tool that will lead people into victorious Christian living and thus a willingness to serve in ministry. The church leaders hope against hope that disciples will be multiplied and the talent pool expanded. Yet what all began with great promise turns to disappointment when only a small percentage of the congregation signs up for the program. Too often it is the already overcommitted who respond. Thus the saints get recycled one more time. The size of the ministry base is substantially the same as it was prior to the promising program. Figure 6.1 depicts this approach.

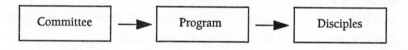

Figure 6.1. Program-based discipling

Missing from this approach is the priority of relationship. I oppose neither curricula,[2] complete with sequenced knowledge, skills acquisition, spiritual disciplines and doctrinal content, nor systems, but for transformation to occur this must all be processed in the context of a relational commitment. Jesus serves as our model. He said to those who would be his disciples, "Follow me and I will make you fish for people" (Mark 1:17). In association with me, Jesus says, I will provide what you will need to fulfill the call I place on your life. This same relational emphasis needs to be at the heart of our disciple-making strategy (see figure 6.2).

What we have failed to appreciate is the power of invitation to be with others on an intimate basis over time. My challenge to the church and Christian community is to return to the primacy of this invitation as we walk together toward maturity in Christ. When I consider initiating a new discipling relationship, prayer to discern the persons the Lord would place on my heart precedes it. Jesus took the initiative to call his disciples to himself after spending the night in prayer; discipling relationships should be formed on the basis of a prayerful invitation by the one initiating the discipling relationship. In offering the invitation to potential partners, I say something to the effect of, "Will you join me, walk with me as we grow together as disciples of Christ? I would like to invite you to meet with me and one other person weekly for the purpose of becoming all that the Lord intended us to be. As I was praying about this relationship, the Lord has drawn me to you." I always want the person to whom I am offering this invitation to know that he or she is not an individual who I have blindly chosen out of the church directory but someone the Lord has laid on my heart with a settled conviction over time. In chapter nine we will reflect on the qualities one might look for in a discipling partner.

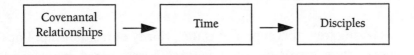

Figure 6.2. Relationship-based discipling

How does this approach differ from the usual church program? Instead of inviting people to a program or class for which they sign up, attend and complete their assignments, they are invited into a relationship of mutual love, transparency and accountability. Of course, discipling relationships contain programmatic elements, such as a curriculum, but the relational dynamics are primary. How does a relationship differ from a program? Let's contrast relationship with the four characteristics of program previously identified. First, discipling relationships are marked by intimacy, whereas programs tend to be focused on information. Alicia Britt Cole captures

124

this difference between program and relationship: "Program was safer, more controllable, and reproducible—less risky, less messy, less intrusive. It seemed easier to give someone an outline than an hour, a well-worn book than a window into our humanity. How easy it is to substitute informing people for investing in people, to confuse organizing people with actually discipling people. Life is not the offspring of program or paper. Life is the offspring of life. Jesus prioritized shoulder-to-shoulder mentoring because His prize was much larger than information; it was integration."[3]

Second, discipling relationships involve full, mutual responsibility of the participants, whereas programs have one or a few who do on behalf of the many. In a discipling relationship the partners equally share responsibility for preparation, self-disclosure and an agenda of change. This is not about one person being the insightful teacher, and the others being the learners who take in the insights of one whose wisdom far exceeds their own. Maturity levels in Christ will vary, but the basic assumption is that in the give and take of relationships, the one who is the teacher and the one who is taught can vary from moment to moment.

Third, discipling relationships are customized to the unique growth process of the individuals, whereas programs emphasize synchronization and regimentation. A program usually has a defined length. You commit to ten weeks, and then you are done. Often churches follow the academic calendar, beginning a program in September when school starts and completing it in June in time for summer vacation. A discipling relationship cannot be confined by such artificial constraints. Discipling relationships necessarily vary in length of time, because no two people grow at the same speed. It is not a matter of a lock-step march through the curriculum but an individualized approach that takes into account the unique growth issues of those involved.

For example, in one of my recent discipling relationships, Mike had come to Christ at age fifty with a minimal church background.

He had spent his career running his own golf-course architectural firm. Mike was full of all the questions of a new convert: Why do the innocent suffer? What is the fate of those who had never heard of Christ? And so on. We took the time to chase down what to others might be considered rabbit trails, whereas for Mike they were genuine inquiries of a hungry new follower. Another Mike in the same group was at middle age. His life agenda had shifted from business success to life significance. He was seeking to discern whether he had a vocational call to professional ministry after a career as a commercial real estate developer. We often set aside the curricular focus of the day to listen to the inner ruminations that went with Mike's yearning for a different focus in his life. Though we followed the structure of a discipling curriculum, the relationship always remained paramount. Programs have a prescribed length; discipling relationships don't. Relationships adjust to the needs and dynamics of what is happening in the lives of the people at the moment.

Fourth, discipling relationships focus accountability around life change, whereas programs focus accountability around content. Growth into Christlikeness is the ultimate goal. The measure of accountability in programs tends to be observable behaviors such as memorizing Scripture, completing the required weekly reading and practicing spiritual disciplines. In a discipling relationship the accountability focuses on learning to observe or "obey everything that [Jesus has] commanded" (Matthew 28:19). For example, there is a huge difference between knowing that Jesus taught that we are to love our enemies and loving our enemies. Discipling relationships are centered on incorporating the life of Jesus in all we are in the context of all that we do.

THE ATTRACTIVENESS OF RELATIONSHIPS

Invitations to programs seem impersonal. A program seems to be something the church tries to get people to come to for their good. An invitation to relationship, by contrast, is experienced very differently. In an impersonal world, people hunger for intimacy, personal care, deep friendship and spiritual bonding. This is particularly true for men. Studies have shown that men generally have acquaintances but few, if any, intimate friends. Two out of ten males seem to have meaningful, open and safe relationships in which both parties trust and are committed to each other. In contrast, six out of ten women enjoy this type of relationship.[4] When men are invited to join two others to explore what it means to follow Jesus, I find a motivating hunger.

One of the men in a church I served spoke for many when he wrote,

> For many years I had been searching for a safe place in which I could explore, with a group of other guys, the questions and issues that were coming up in my walk with the Lord. On earlier occasions, I had enjoyed Bible studies that were aimed at either couples or larger groups of guys. Neither one of these settings had really stretched me to examine my faith in a personal way and find out who I was in Christ. As a result of this spiritual hunger, I began looking for a small group of fellow believers who wanted to develop a deeper relationship with our Lord through a regular study of His word. In short, I was looking for some men with whom I could be honest, accountable, and vulnerable.[5]

BUILD SLOWLY, BUILD SOLIDLY

By giving relationship priority, we need to change our short-cut approaches to making disciples. Underlying the programmatic mindset is a view that disciples can be made quickly. We are always looking for an instantaneous solution to our recruiting problems or growing people in Christ. Robert Coleman puts the key issue in stark focus: "One must decide where he wants his ministry to count—in the momentary applause of popular recognition (program splash) or in the reproduction of his life in a few chosen ones who will carry on his work after he has gone? Really, it is a question of which generation we are living for."[6]

The temptation to which we have succumbed with such regularity is to seek "the momentary applause of popular recognition." We judge our success by the number of people in the worship center. We hold a pastor's Bible study as the means to getting God's Word into people. Or we adopt the latest program that seems to produce results somewhere else. Behind these efforts is the mentality of the instantaneous.

Coleman, following Jesus' model, points us toward building slowly and building solidly. A significant portion of a leader's time should be given to a "few chosen ones who will carry on their work after they are gone." This means having enough vision to think small. An effective builder of people looks ahead five to seven years for the discipleship results. Yet our inability to delay gratification is a major contributing factor to our discipleship deficit. At a seminary in Manila I spoke to Filipino pastors about the need to have a long-term vision of disciple making. As I was speaking, I became aware of a murmur spreading through the class. I stopped my lecture and said, "What did I say? What's going on?" They explained to me that in the uncertainty of their political climate, when a regime change can occur at any moment, thinking long term seemed laughable. I pushed back. I said, "You will, most likely, be pastors in the same locations as you are seven years from now, so you might as well invest for the long haul." It appears that thinking long term is not any more common in the West than it is in the Philippines.

In the model I will propose, three people journey together for a year to a year and a half while they grow toward maturity and being equipped to disciple others. As this relationship comes to a close, the challenge comes to each person to invite two others into the same walk of faith and then reproduce, and so on. Over the five- to seven-year period of multiplying discipleship triads, it is common to have eighty to a hundred or more people who have been carefully groomed in the context of an intimate relationship. This number of self-initiating, reproducing disciples has a tremendous impact on the climate of a ministry. It takes only 10 to 20 percent of a congregation to set the tone for the whole. Invest in those who will set the pace for the rest. At the same time, one's leadership base is greatly expanded. Key leaders who are willing to assume responsibility for ministry or initiate new ministries come from this discipleship harvest. Most of us never see that kind of fruit, because we do not have that kind of vision. We are too oriented to short-term results, and therefore we try to create shortcuts that don't produce the growth we want. We consistently serve churches made up of people who are overgrown spiritual children because we have not focused on the principle of building slowly but building solidly.

DISCIPLING DEFINED

What is included in a discipling relationship? At the heart of discipling is a relationship in which one or more believers assist or invest in each other in order to grow to maturity in Christ. Bill Hull defines discipling as "the intentional training of disciples, with accountability, on the basis of loving relationship."[7] The International Consultation on Discipleship established a working definition of discipleship that contains the elements of discipling: "We define Christian discipleship as a process *that takes place within accountable relationships over a period of time* for the purpose of bringing believers to spiritual maturity in Christ."[8] The distinctive nature of discipling is that it involves a relational investment intended to create an atmosphere of growth to maturity in Christ.

My working definition of discipling underlies the model of discipling relationship under consideration. "Discipling is an intentional relationship in which we walk alongside other disciples in order to encourage, equip, and challenge one another in love to grow toward maturity in Christ. This includes equipping the disciple to teach others as well."[9]

129

Michael Wilkins has written, "Our choice of terminology determines the kind of expectations that we communicate to people."[10] Our definition of discipling will determine the model that we use for how disciples are made. Since this definition of discipling contains the guiding vision for the nature of the discipling relationship, it is important to understand what is being stated and how this view of discipling is distinguished from other approaches.

Intentional relationship. At a most basic level, "intentional" means that the discipling partners will meet on a regular time schedule, preferably weekly. "Let's get together when we can" is at the other end of the spectrum from intentional. "Intentional" also implies purposeful. A relationship is established for the purpose of "growing together toward maturity in Christ." There is a covenantal character to the relationship. The parties commit themselves to mutually agreed vows that give shape to the relationship. Relationship, or being with one another, is the primary means through which Christlikeness will be produced.

Walk alongside other disciples. This phrase is carefully chosen to convey that this approach to disciple making is nonhierarchical. The intent is to create a mutual, egalitarian interchange, where life rubs up against life. For reasons I will strongly press in chapter seven, this definition proposes a peer mentoring approach to discipling rather than "a more experienced follower of Christ shares with a newer believer"[11] or "teacher-student relationship."[12]

Three qualities characterize this reciprocal discipling relationship.

First, in discipling relationships we *encourage* one another. We need safe places where we are free to explore who we are in Christ in a positive, grace-giving environment. The Holy Spirit is described as the *parakletos* (often translated "encourager") who comes alongside to help. Discipling partners are the Holy Spirit's instruments, used to affirm all that is special in another as God releases us to be his unique creations.

Second, growing into Christlikeness involves *equipping* our daily lives with disciplines that place us in the presence of Christ's shaping influence. The word *equip* implies that part of the process will include practicing skills, disciplines, behaviors and patterns that give structure to being a follower of Jesus. Included in transformation is the reordering of habits.

Finally, in the context of a covenantal relationship, there will come times when our partners *challenge* us for failing to follow through on commitments we have made or strongly urge us to take risks. Just as I challenged Eric to pursue a mission opportunity in the midst of his intended world tour, so there will be times when others need to challenge us. Challenge implies that there is accountability rooted in a mutual covenant. A frightening step for most of us is to invite others to have authority over our lives.

In love. It is important to wrap all of what is done in the discipling relationship in love for those whom we are with on the journey. Love and trust are inseparable. As soon as we suspect that someone is attempting to control us or speak to us in anger in order to punish or harm, then we will become guarded and withdraw. Love is the womb in which Christ can be formed in us. Chicks best emerge from the egg to new life when they have received the warmth of a nesting hen.

To grow toward maturity in Christ. The goal of a discipling relationship is to become whole, complete or mature in Christ. This means that no one partner has arrived, but all are on a common journey toward being fully grown in Christ. A reason for the stress on peer accountability is that no one person can serve as a complete model for another. In fact, a sign of maturity is the ability to learn from the least likely source.

Equipping to teach others. The goal is reproduction. Included within our understanding of maturity is that the disciple has internalized the value of multiplication and gained the confidence and ability to lead someone to Christ and walk alongside that person toward Christlikeness.

DISCIPLING INCARNATED

A number of years ago I received one of those letters that redeems all the disappointments in ministry. I share a portion of this letter because the author illustrates so powerfully the importance of long-term discipling relationships. My first ministry position out of seminary was with college students at the University of Pittsburgh. The church I served was located across the street from the student dorms. We had developed a fairly extensive outreach to some three hundred students attending our midweek service. At the center of the ministry was a leadership team of about forty students who led outreach Bible studies on the college campus and were being discipled by our five full-time staff. The letter I received was from a former student at the university who was a freshman at the time I was called from Pittsburgh to serve a church in California. I barely knew this student, yet she wrote to commend the ministry model she had experienced at the University of Pittsburgh. What makes this letter all the more compelling is the time lag between when I left this ministry and when she wrote. My departure from Pittsburgh to California occurred in March 1977, and her letter is dated April 1985.

Dear Greg,

My name is Jane Smith [not her real name]. I was just starting to get involved in the church fellowship when you were called to California. I was so impressed with the few times I heard you teach, but more than anything else I was drawn into the love that the fellowship had for you and each other. To an outsider at the time, like myself, one saw such a deep love that I know was prayerfully developed. The term discipleship was living.

Long after you left, your leadership materials were being used—I was trained by [she mentions three student leaders] . . . who were a part of the inner circle that I admired and the Lord used in my life.

After graduating from the University of Pittsburgh with degrees in child development/child care, my husband and I were led to start a Christian center [in Pennsylvania]. The Lord has done miracles step after step in this ministry, and we're so excited about it! We started with a preschool program and now have started a Christian school, adding a grade each year.

We feel that by applying biblical principles and models that we can minister to families in the area. In any case, because of the model I experienced at Pitt, the center is focusing on small, quality, long-term relationships with families.

Now, the reason I'm writing—I realize now the commitment you had at Pitt and how much time and effort you so selflessly poured into those guys. I appreciate you and your gifts because I feel like I am the fruit of your fruit! And praise the Lord more fruit is being produced! I appreciate your model because of our ministry, and how easy it is to give yourself out and spread too thin and not accomplish much. If you ever question the Lord about your work at Pitt—please think of me and know how much the Lord used you there. So . . . I just wanted to say thanks!

P.S. I guess you will understand this letter—I just pray that someday someone will write to me expressing their faith in our Lord, and that perhaps my obedience was somehow related to their growth.

Jane underscores all the points I have been trying to stress in this chapter. Let's highlight her insights.

The term discipleship was living. In the community of believers Jane saw the embodiment of discipleship through the love of the community for its leaders and for each other. Love was the magnet that drew her to this body. Jesus had something to say about this: "By this everyone will know that you are my disciples, if you have love for one another" (John 13:35). Jane observed this truth in

Christian community probably long before she read it in her Bible.

Trained by members of the inner circle. There was an inner circle, a part of the leadership core. The leaders met every Wednesday evening for training and support in their ministry. Each member of the student team was being discipled and encouraged by staff as they led outreach Bible studies on campus and had their few in whom they also invested. In this setting these were junior and senior college students, whom Jane admired and who reproduced themselves in her.

Long after you left. A discipling or training model has a much greater chance of outliving a primary leader than does one built around a leader's personality. The test of leadership is what happens after the leader moves on to his or her next ministry. The ministry was infused with a philosophy of discipleship reproduction, which was not dependent upon me. Jane was a freshman at the time of my departure. I had a minimal relationship with her, yet the relational and developmental structure was in place to carry her through her four years of college.

Because of the model I learned. In establishing a ministry to families, Jane and her husband had decided to focus on "small, quality and long-term relationships." I could not have picked three better adjectives to describe the discipling process. She and her husband had chosen depth over breadth.

The fruit of your fruit. I have publicly and privately read this letter perhaps fifty times or more in the last seventeen years, and I never come to that line without a catch in my throat and moisture in my eyes. Here is a young woman with whom I had almost no personal relationship. Yet she recognized that the discipling chain had passed through the generations and that she was in a sense my spiritual granddaughter. What a joy it is to know that the reproduction does take place when those whom you have discipled have caught the vision and have the skill to disciple others.

Jane captures what has been the fatal flaw in ministry and has been a major cause for undiscipled believers: how easy it is to give yourself out and spread too thin and not accomplish much. This is the epitaph that could be written over the life of many a pastor or Christian leader. In our attempt to be equally available to all and avoid being accused of having favorites, are there "small, quality, long-term relationships" where people truly capture in-depth what discipleship is about?

It really is about having enough vision to think small. This requires that we shift our way of thinking and acting to produce lasting fruit in key individuals, who will in turn teach others. We must exorcise the instantaneous from our thinking. Put off the old ways of being all things to all people. Realize that one of the key leadership roles is to have a few at all times in whom we are investing, preferably weekly, who are being brought to maturity in Christ in a relational context. The results of this longer-term strategy will be a broadening leadership base of self-initiating disciples, multiplication of fruit beyond our initial efforts and a ministry that will long outlive us. "Essentially, the pastor's first priority is to so invest himself or herself in a few other persons that they also become disciplers and ministers of Jesus Christ. It is to so give oneself to others and to the work of discipling that the New Testament norm of plural leadership or eldership becomes a reality in the local congregation. In other words, it is to bring the ministry of all of God's people to functioning practical reality."[13]

If the mantra regarding the value of real estate is "location, location, location," then the core ingredient in making disciples is "relationship, relationship, relationship." In chapter seven we will see how these relationships can add the component of multiplication, and in chapter eight we look at three key ingredients in the relationship that create the atmosphere for transformation.

7

MULTIPLICATION
Through the Generations

The question that has served as the driving force behind this book is, How can we grow self-initiating, reproducing, fully devoted followers of Jesus Christ? The most befuddling challenge contained in this question and the conundrum few have solved centers around reproducing. Perhaps an even greater challenge than growing fully devoted followers of Christ is growing fully devoted followers who reproduce. Reproduction is the key to fulfilling the Great Commission, "Go therefore and make disciples of all nations" (Matthew 28:19).

Any credible definition of discipling should contain within it the concept of reproduction. Gary Kunhe has written, "Discipleship training is the spiritual work of developing spiritual maturity and spiritual *reproductiveness* in the life of a Christian."[1] Kunhe says this same thing from the angle of one who is setting the disciple-making pace: "A multiplier is a disciple who is training his spiritual children to *reproduce* themselves."[2] We must raise the bar so that there is a new normative expectation. To train a disciple is to train a reproducer.

Along these lines of reproduction, you have likely seen the charts that compare evangelism by *addition* to evangelism by *multiplication* (see figure 7.1).

YEAR	EVANGELIST	DISCIPLER
1	365	2
2	730	4
3	1095	8
4	1460	16
5	1825	32
6	2190	64
7	2555	128
8	2920	256
9	3285	512
10	3650	1,024
11	4015	2,048
12	4380	4,096
13	4745	8,192
14	5110	16,384
15	5475	32,768
16	5840	65,536

Figure 7.1. Evangelistic addition vs. discipleship multiplication

To interpret the chart, let us suppose an evangelist operated out of an addition strategy. If an evangelist won one person a day to Christ for the next sixteen years (365 per year) there would be 5,840 decisions for Christ. If that same evangelist took a multiplication or reproductive approach, the tactics would be quite different. Instead of continuing to win one person a day, the evangelist would become a discipler. The discipler would win one person per year and spend the year discipling that person to maturity in Christ, which includes reproduction. At the end of that first year the same discipler would win another person and follow the same process. The multiplication occurs when the person discipled during the first year is also able to bring another to Christ and walk with him or her so that new convert is capable of reproducing as well.

The numbers after two years of multiplication are not very remarkable. Only four fully devoted followers would have been produced. By comparison the evangelist has continued to add one person a day over the two years and is up to 730 new converts. But if the multiplication approach (discipler) were to go on for sixteen years, there would be 65,536 followers of Christ, each of whom has been equipped to reproduce themselves. After sixteen years the addition approach would have yielded only 5,840 followers. The addition approach makes it the responsibility of the lone evangelist to win and nurture. Follow-up, or grounding the new believers in this model, becomes a numerical impossibility, whereas with the multiplication model, follow-up is built in.

These multiplication tables are impressive on paper. Carry them out for thirty years, and you will quickly see we can have easily discipled this entire planet a few times over and spread to nearby galaxies. As impressive as these addition or multiplication charts are, in my experience they don't work in real life. For a couple of decades I lived with the frustration that I was not seeing those in whom I was investing equipped to disciple others. My usual approach was to meet with someone one-on-one on a weekly basis. My hope was to encourage a deepening faithfulness to Christ and to empower the individual to reproduce in another, and so on, thus multiplying effectiveness. Our agenda would include mutual sharing about the growing edges of our faith; learning and practicing the basic spiritual disciplines, such as the devotional elements of prayer and Bible study and Scripture memory; exploring the implications of obedience to Christ in the spheres of family, work, church or inner struggles; studying a foundational book such as John Stott's *Basic Christianity;* and coaching the person in a church-related ministry. But there was no multiplication.

I was stymied. For fifteen to twenty years I labored with a discipleship model that amply demonstrated to me the current popular definition of insanity. Insanity, it has been said, is doing the same thing over and over again and expecting different results. I thought what I needed to do was refine or improve the same thing I was doing. If I would try harder, pray more regularly, refine my approach here and there, then the results would be different. Multiplication charts acted as law, condemning me in my failure where others (those who publish the multiplication charts) must be succeeding. After all these years I have concluded that perhaps the model I was pursuing was faulty. To paraphrase Dallas Willard, perhaps the reason I was getting these results was not in spite of my approach to discipling but because of it.

I was forced to ask some probing questions that are perhaps the same ones you are asking. Why don't we see more reproduction? What obstacles get in the way? Is it a matter of a low commitment? Is it the fault of leaders who are afraid to ask for more? Have we succumbed to the comfort of Western consumerism and therefore even our Christianity is only about what God can do for us? These are contributing factors. In chapter two we looked at a number of causes for the low estate of discipleship. But here my question is more focused: What are the barriers to reproduction? Why don't even our intentional discipleship models seem to produce multiplication?

Some fifteen years ago I stumbled on a change of approach that has led to a 75 percent reproduction rate in an ever-growing network of church-based disciple-making strategy. My problem, in my estimation, was that I had become transfixed by a biblical icon, which fueled a nonreproducible practical model.

THE USUAL BIBLICAL MODEL (PAUL AND TIMOTHY)

When it comes to a biblical paradigm or relationship that serves as the basis for our understanding of discipling, what is brought forth as exhibit A? Paul and Timothy. These two are linked together as the prototypical unit. Preachers regularly urge every Paul to have a Timothy, or even more commonly for every Timothy to seek out a Paul to be a mentor. Our definitions of discipling are generally influenced by the unspoken assumption that the Paul-Timothy model is the universal paradigm. Paul Stanley and J. Robert Clinton support this one-on-one model of the more mature believer discipling the less mature: "Discipling is a process in which a more experienced follower of Christ shares with a newer believer the commitment, understanding and basic skills necessary to know and obey Jesus Christ as Lord."[3] Lurking in the background of Keith Phillip's definition is the Paul-Timothy model. "Christian discipleship is a teacher-student relationship . . . in which the teacher reproduces the fullness of life he has in Christ in the student so well, so that the student is able to train others to teach others."[4]

In linking Paul and Timothy as *the* biblical model, assumptions are made as to what kind of relationship this should entail:

- Older person with a younger person (like a father-son relationship)

- More spiritually mature with less spiritually mature

- Teacher-student relationship (learned with the unlearned)

- More experienced with the less experienced

- One in authority over one under authority

THE USUAL MODEL OF DISCIPLE MAKING

Because of the imprint of the Paul-Timothy model, we unquestioningly assume the one-on-one relationship as our reference point in discipling relationships. But with the hindsight of seventeen years of discipling in triads, the following are my reflections on some of the limitations of the one-to-one discipling dynamics.

In the one-on-one relationship, the discipler carries the responsibility for the spiritual welfare of another. The discipler is like the mother bird that goes out to scavenge for worms to feed to her babies. With their mouths wide open, the babes wait in their nest for the mother bird to return. The discipler is cast in the role of passing on his or her vast knowledge to the one with limited knowledge. This pressures the discipler to perform and be the focal point in the relationship. In this model, in order to disciple another, one must have arrived at some undefined state of spiritual perfection. Unwittingly we have created a role for which few will perceive they are qualified to apply. Instead of the discipler enjoying a freedom or ability to be oneself, there is a self-consciousness born of a false perfectionism.

The one-on-one relationship sets up a hierarchy that tends to result in dependency. As appreciative as the Timothies might be, people in the receiving position will often not be able to see themselves in the giving position. After all, the dynamic created is that they are the young, immature ones being taught. They are there to receive from the fount of wisdom of the one who has walked longer in the faith. The gulf between the Paul and the Timothy is only exacerbated when the relationship is between pastor and parishioner. There is already an unbridgeable clergy/laity chasm created by ordination. Pastors are qualified to disciple others (so states the conventional wisdom), because they have years of biblical and theological training and the vocation to go with it.

One-on-one relationships limit the interchange or dialogue. I liken the one-to-one discourse to a ping-pong match. It is back and forth, with the discipler under pressure to keep the ball in play. The conversation and dialogue must constantly progress to some higher plane. As a discipler I found that I did not listen as carefully as I should have, because I was thinking about some wise counsel or insight I might provide given my role. In other words, the dialogue is often not a dynamic interchange, limited by the number of participants.

One-on-one relationships also create a one-model approach. The primary influence on a new disciple becomes a single person. This in itself can be limiting and tends to skew the development of the disciple. The parameters of the discipling experience are defined by the strengths and weaknesses of one individual.

Finally, and of vital importance, the one-on-one model does not generally reproduce. If it does, it is rare. Only self-confident, inwardly motivated persons can break the dependency and become self-initiating and reproducing.

We have inadvertently held up a hierarchical, positional model of discipling that is nontransferable. As long as there is the sense that one person is over another by virtue of superior spiritual authority, however that is measured, few people will see themselves as qualified to disciple others. We may tout this as a multiplication method, but it contains the seeds of its own destruction.

As a result of my experience, I propose a nonhierarchical model that views discipling as a mutual process of peer mentoring. In order to avoid the dependency trap, the relationship needs to be seen as side by side rather than one person having authority or position over another.

THE ALTERNATIVE BIBLICAL MODEL
A biblical alternative to the Paul-Timothy model will serve as the basis for a side-by-side relational approach to disciple making. Though the relationship between Barnabas and Paul ended with them parting company in a dispute over Barnabas's cousin, John Mark (Acts 15:39), it still serves as "iron sharpens iron" peer discipling that I find healthy and consistent with Paul's view of his relational partnership in mission. What we will observe as we track Barnabas and Paul's connection through the book of Acts is that these two constantly change who is in the lead position. The changes depend on their gifts and the ministry circumstance.

Barnabas makes his first appearance at the end of Acts 4. We discover that Barnabas is a nickname given to him by the apostles, meaning "son of encouragement," because he so embodied this attribute (Acts 4:36). He was born Joseph from Cyprus and was a Levite. Barnabas had sold a piece of property and entrusted the proceeds to the apostles so they might use the money for the needy in the church community. The next mention of Barnabas occurs in Acts 9, when he becomes linked with the firebrand Saul—turned apostle Paul. The disciples in Jerusalem were rightly skeptical of Paul's conversion. They feared it was a ruse or masquerade feigned to infiltrate the ranks of the apostles. It was Barnabas who vouched for the genuineness of Paul's life change and witnessed how he had put his life on the line in Damascus, speaking boldly about Jesus (Acts 9:27).

Barnabas and Paul parted company for a considerable time until they were reunited in Antioch (Acts 11:19-30). Barnabas had been sent by the headquarters in Jerusalem to investigate the strange rumors that not only had the Jews received the grace of God in Antioch, but the Gentiles as well. Having gained a reputation for being able to spot the genuine article, Barnabas was their man. Barnabas affirmed that the same manifestations of grace rested upon these Gentile believers as was evidenced in the chosen people. After sizing up the situation, Barnabas recognized that the teaching task was greater than he could handle by himself. Though years had passed by now, he remembered the call of God upon Paul, who was commissioned by the Lord to be an apostle to the Gentiles. Barnabas tracked Paul down in his hometown of Tarsus; Paul had exorcised his legalistic Pharisaism and replaced it by freedom in grace theology. Barnabas was the tool that the Lord used to get Paul into the game.

Barnabas and Paul labored side by side in Antioch until the Holy Spirit spoke to the worshiping leaders, confirming that they were to be sent on what we now call Paul's first missionary journey (Acts 13:1-2). It is interesting to observe how the order of the names—

Paul and Barnabas, Barnabas and Paul—change in the varying circumstances of their work. While Paul emerges as the primary spokesperson, it is evident that he does not eclipse Barnabas. Sometimes it is Barnabas and Paul (Acts 13:2, 7; 14:12, 14; 15:12, 25) and sometimes it is Paul and Barnabas (Acts 13:42, 46, 50; 14:1; 15:2, 22, 35).

The point of the shift from Paul-Timothy to Barnabas-Paul as the biblical model for disciple making is the need to change from a hierarchical approach that creates dependency to a peer mentoring model that has much more promise of empowering multiplication. At this point you may rightly object, *But what about modeling? Isn't it important that someone who has walked longer in the faith be an example and teacher for those who are just beginning? Haven't you spent an entire section of this book helping us see that Jesus invested in a few and that his life was the primary means of influence used to shape the Twelve? You have told us that Paul even had the audacity to say, "Imitate me as I imitate Christ." Now you seem to be backing away from modeling being the foundation of disciple making.*

What I am saying is that placing the discipler in positional authority over the disciplee is not necessary for modeling to occur. Let's return to the examples of Jesus and Paul. Upon what was Jesus' authority based? Certainly not any recognized manmade position he held. The Greek word for authority is *exousia*, which means "out of being." Jesus spoke as one having authority, not as the scribes and Pharisees. Jesus' authority was recognized in the ring of truth of his words, backed by the consistent quality of his life and underscored with a demonstration of power. The only human title Jesus acknowledged was Rabbi. Jesus did not have authority because of his association with a recognized rabbinical school or the *imprimatur* of a highly regarded rabbi. Paul's authority was not so much in his position as apostle but in his passionate desire to die to himself so that Christ would come alive in him. The qualities in his life, not the credentials he held, made his life worth imitating.

The person leading a discipling triad need not hold a position of authority, except to be the keeper of the covenant to which the group members have mutually agreed. Authority or impact is more a matter of function than of position. In other words, in the relational context, influence will naturally occur within the relationship. The depth of one's spiritual life and insight, the evident passion to serve Christ, the application of Scripture to life, will all naturally flow out in the dynamic interchange. Authority is placed in the mutual covenant to which the participants agree. If the qualifying mark of those who are involved in the triad is the desire to be all that Christ wants them to be, whatever their starting point—pre-Christian to veteran—then there is an environment for transformation.

THE ALTERNATIVE MODEL OF DISCIPLE MAKING

As the alternative to the one-on-one model, I propose a threesome that I call a triad as the ideal size for a disciple-making group. Though I have convened groups of four and find them adequate, the group of three appears to maximize the transformative dynamics in a discipleship relationship (see chap. 8).

It was not my great foresight that led me to change from the one-to-one to a triad. As I mentioned in the introduction, it came as a result of a ministry experiment in an academic program. I had written an earlier version of the curriculum now entitled *Discipleship Essentials* and wanted to test its usefulness. Since this experiment became the basis for a final project for a doctor of ministry degree, my project adviser suggested that I try it out in different contexts in order to examine the variable dynamics. We agreed that I would use the material in the traditional one-on-one mode, in a small group of ten, and also in a group of three. I was caught off guard with the life-giving dynamics I experienced in the triads.

How could adding just one person change the entire feel of what happened in that relationship? The goal had not changed. The goal was still to see the Lord grow self-initiating, reproducing, fully devoted followers of Jesus. The only difference was the direction and structure provided by a curriculum and the addition of one individual, yet it all seemed so much more alive!

Here is my best take on why triads are energizing, joy-filled and reproductive.

There is a shift from unnatural pressure to natural participation of the discipler. When a third person is added, there is a shift from the discipler as focal point to a group process. The discipler in this setting is a fellow participant. Though the discipler is the convener of the triad, the participants quickly become one of three on the journey together toward maturity in Christ. The responsibility that comes from being the focal point is lessened, since the emphasis is on mutuality. The discipler prepares and interacts with the content as a peer rather than as an authority whose insight is to be weighted more heavily because of the leadership position.

There is a shift from hierarchical to relational. The triad naturally creates a come-alongside mutual journey. The focus is not so much upon the discipler as it is upon Christ as the one toward whom all are directing their lives. I found even as a pastor that, though the relationship may have started with a consciousness that I was the Bible answer-man because of my title and training, within the first few weeks the threesome allowed me to be another disciple with fellow disciples who were attempting together to follow Jesus. A significant part of the discipling relationship is to share our personal challenges of faithfulness. When my partners saw that I too was having to deal with the real stuff of life, the polished halo faded and I was allowed to be a real person.

There is a shift from dialogue to dynamic interchange. In my initial experiment with triads, I often came away from those times saying to myself, *What made that interchange so alive and dynamic?*

The presence of the Holy Spirit seemed palpable. Life and energy marked the exchange. As I have come to understand group dynamics, one-on-one is not a group. It is only as you add a third that you have the first makings of a group.

With one-on-one, there are only four possible combinations of communication. Each individual has a unique perspective and an opinion about the other person's perspective. When you add a third party, the number of possible interplays of communication increases to ten. Each of the three persons has two relationships (six); then each person has a relationship with the other two as a pair (three), thus making nine possible configurations. But there is a group personality, which is the tenth and most dynamic aspect of the threesome. The addition of a third personality multiplies the possible configurations of communication and creates a corporate personality.

There is a shift from limited input to wisdom in numbers. The book of Proverbs speaks of the wisdom that comes from many counselors (Proverbs 15:22). To this end I have often found it life-giving to have people at varied maturity levels. Often those who may be perceived as younger or less mature in the faith provide great wisdom or a fresh spark of life. Ken was perhaps the least likely source of spiritual inspiration in one of my triads. His partners were me, a pastor, and Glen, an ex-Baptist pastor, whose knowledge of Scripture exceeded mine. Ken, a retired dentist, had come to a warm relationship with Christ well into his sixties, but he lacked confidence, especially in his knowledge of Scripture. In the first weeks of our sessions, Ken slumped in his chair with his head bowed. The bottom edge of a discipleship workbook was propped on his lap and hugged to his chest as if he were afraid for anyone to see what he had written. He reminded me of a third grader who did not want to make eye contact with the teacher in order to avoid getting called on.

Only a few weeks into our relationship Ken was diagnosed with cancer and had to begin weeklong in-hospital regimens of chemo-therapy every third week. So every third week our discipleship sessions shifted from my office to the chapel on the hospital floor where Ken was receiving his treatments. Far from this adversity setting Ken back, it seemed to open up a surge of God's grace flowing into his life. The once insecure neophyte was now eagerly teaching us about how God's presence was available in times of testing. It wasn't long before Ken had become the unofficial chaplain on the hospital floor, moving from room to room pulling his drip bag behind him. His demeanor radiated the warmth of Christ's love. The teachers (Glen and I) were now being taught. We were sitting at Ken's feet, hearing a man speak wisdom beyond his Christian years.

There is a shift from addition to multiplication. For the better part of two decades, I have observed an approximate 75 percent reproduction rate through the triad model of disciple making. One of the joyful memories seared into my brain was my last Sunday in 1988 as associate pastor at the church where I first developed a network of triad relationships. As I was leaving the church property that Sunday, I ran into Kathy on the patio under our sprawling Morton Bay fig. She cradled in her arms the 8-1/2" by 11" spiral-bound notebook I had titled *A Disciple's Guide for Today* (the precursor to *Discipleship Essentials*). She giddily told me that Kay had invited her into a discipleship triad, which was going to begin that next week. My first thought was, *What a joy it is to know that a ministry of discipling and reproduction now has a life of its own and is going to continue to multiply long after old "what's-his-name" is forgotten.* That joy was further enhanced since I had nothing to do with discipling Kay, who had invited Kathy into her next triad. As senior pastor at my last church, I saw the same intergenerational reproduction. In a discipleship newsletter we called *Discipleship Bytes* (this is the Silicon Valley), the names were listed of all who were currently participating or had participated in this intentional discipleship process. By that time, well over a hundred people had completed and reproduced themselves in the next generation. My heart was warmed when I saw on the list spiritual grandchildren and great-grandchildren who were far removed from the original triads that got the whole process going.

In summary, a triad encourages multiplication because it minimizes the hierarchical dimensions and maximizes a peer mentoring model. By providing a discipleship curriculum specifically designed for this intimate relationship, it creates a simple, reproducible structure that almost any growing believer can lead. Leadership in these groups can be rotated early on, since the size makes for an informal interchange and the curriculum provides a guide to follow.

APPROPRIATE ONE-TO-ONE MENTORING RELATIONSHIPS

In my discipling workshops, at this point I often find the participants objecting to my perceived attack on the one-on-one model. People will push back with stories of how their lives were meaningfully influenced by another in a long-term relationship. Their implicit question is, How could this be a deficient model if I have had such a positive experience? It is not my intent to dismiss as deficient anyone's positive one-on-one experience of discipleship or to say that there are not valuable contexts for the one-to-one relationship. Paul Stanley and J. Robert Clinton have done a great service in identifying different types of "intensive mentoring" relationships.[5]

Providing a thumbnail description of these relationships will help us understand the niche of discipling on which this book is focused as well as affirm the appropriate context for one-on-one mentoring. There are three other types of mentoring relationships where the one-to-one is the appropriate context: spiritual guide or director, coach and sponsor.

SPIRITUAL GUIDE

Stanley and Clinton define a spiritual guide as "a godly, mature, follower of Christ who shares knowledge, skills and basic philosophy on what it means to increasingly realize Christlikeness in all areas of life."[6] Whereas the discipling relationship is meant to lay the foundations and address the basics of discipleship, a spiritual guide or director provides the means to go deeper into the heart and will of God and a context to practice and develop spiritual disciplines. In a discipling relationship one is invited by the discipler. The spiritual guide is sought out by the one who wants guidance.

I have benefited from a one-on-one relationship with a spiritual director. I had moved from the pastorate into an academic setting, and as a result I was struggling with my identity. After twenty-four years I knew who I was as a pastor in a church. But I found myself out of my comfort zone as an administrator of an academic program and a professor in a school. I needed a helpful guide and sounding board to listen to my confusions and ruminations and give me feedback. I sought out a person trained in spiritual direction to help me sense what the Lord was up to in my life. Whereas discipling is a mutual relationship, the relationship with a spiritual director is a one-way street. The spiritual director generally does not open his or her life but prayerfully listens, gives feedback and makes suggestions for how to grow in the ability to discern God's voice in one's life.

COACH

The next intensive one-on-one mentoring role identified by Stanley and Clinton is that of a coach. They define the role of the coach as "providing motivation and imparting skills and application to meet a task or challenge."[7] Coaching is more narrowly focused than discipling, for it relates to specific skills needed for a task and the encouragement needed to grow in those skills. Though discipling involves training in specific skills, such as spiritual disciplines, a coach is sought out for his or her expertise. As with a spiritual guide, the one in need goes in search of the appropriate coach, whereas a discipling relationship comes at the invitation of the discipler.

In my last senior pastorate, an evaluation by the personnel committee determined I needed to improve my skills in supervising staff. As a result, I sought out and established a coaching relationship with a Christian businessman from a neighboring church who had a proven track record in developing the staff in his business. We met approximately every other week over breakfast to cover how to create development plans for each staff member and to do a readiness assessment to be annually presented to the council of elders. I grew in my supervisory skills, but I also received the benefit of his wisdom and the encouragement that I could grow in this area of ministry.

SPONSOR

The last contrasting role of mentoring to discipling that I want to mention is that of sponsor. Stanley and Clinton define a sponsor as "a mentor having credibility and positional or spiritual authority within an organization or network [who] relates to a mentoree not having those resources so as to enable development of the mentoree and the mentoree's influence in the organization."[8] For example, I have acted as sponsor to Karl in the academic program that I directed. Karl came to us after years of successfully administering a sizable engineering firm. His skills far exceeded his initial role in our program. Yet those outside of our office did not readily observe Karl's quiet competence. I set about to trumpet Karl's extensive leadership and administrative skills. Largely based on my endorsement of Karl, it was decided that Karl should become the administrative director, while I moved to academic director. I acted as Karl's sponsor within the organization to maximize the contribution he could make.

The nature of the triad discipling relationship is sharpened by distinguishing it from the one-on-one mentoring relationships of spiritual guide, coach and sponsor. Discipling is foundational, whereas the above-mentioned relationships are more specialized, optional and occasional. A major reason we have not been producing fully devoted followers of Christ is that people have not been intentionally discipled in a manner that is reproducible. Can you imagine the kingdom impact if every believer had the opportunity to be involved in an intensive, year-long relationship with at least two others whose expressed purpose was to grow to become a reproducing disciple of Jesus? Church life would shift from the ministry of professionals to a mobilized body of multipliers.

This more intimate, intentional small-group environment contains within it the elements for transformation to take place. If the goal is to grow self-initiating, reproducing, fully devoted followers of Christ, then this means that we need contexts in which the metamorphosis into Christlikeness can become a lifelong quest. This then places before us the question, What ingredients converge in a triad to make them transformative contexts? It is to this subject we turn our attention in the next chapter.

8

TRANSFORMATION

The Three Necessary Ingredients

Without question, the setting where I have experienced the most accelerated transformation in the lives of believers has been in triads, or small reproducible discipleship groups. I call them the hothouse of Christian growth. Hothouses maximize the environmental conditions so that living things can grow at a rate greater than would exist under normal circumstances. On a recent trip to Alaska my wife and I gaped at daffodils the size of dinner plates and heard stories about five-hundred-pound pumpkins and zucchinis the length of baseball bats. During the summer months in Alaska the sun almost never ceases to shine. Though the growing season is quite short (May through August), the conditions are optimum for accelerated development. This is what happens in a triad. Progress in living the Christian life may have been steady and incremental throughout a believer's life to this point, but with entry into a triad there is a gear shift to warp speed.

Why is this? What are the climatic conditions in a discipleship group of three or four that create the hothouse effect? Three ingredients converge to release the Holy Spirit to bring about a rapid growth toward Christlikeness. These can be summarized in the following biblical principle: When we (1) open our hearts in transparent trust to each other (2) around the truth of God's Word (3) in the spirit of mutual accountability, we are in the Holy Spirit's hothouse of transformation.

Let's look at what is contained in each of these three environmental elements:

CLIMATIC CONDITION ONE: TRANSPARENT TRUST

We return to the fundamental truth that has been the repeated subtheme in this book: Intimate, accountable relationship with other believers is the foundation for growing in discipleship. But what kind of relationship is this? The atmosphere to be fostered in a triad is an ever-increasing openness and transparency. Why is this a necessary condition for change? The extent to which we are willing to reveal to others those areas of our life that need God's transforming touch is the extent to which we are inviting the Holy Spirit to make us new. Our willingness to enter into horizontal or relational intimacy is a statement of our true desire to invite the Lord to make over our lives.

You could rebut this relational challenge by arguing that you already have a transparently honest relationship with God. Your life is an open book to the Lord. "I have nothing to hide," you might say. In your relationship with the Lord you regularly invite the Lord to expose the secrets of your heart, and you hold nothing back from his piercing gaze. Therefore it is nobody else's business what your struggles are with your dark side as long as you are not deceiving God.

Therein lies the problem: deception. Human beings have an almost infinite capacity for self-deception and self-justification. The prophet Jeremiah captured the mystery of the human heart when he wrote, "The heart is devious above all else; it is perverse—who can understand it?" (Jeremiah 17:9). For example, when it comes to human peccadilloes, we tend to be hard on others and soft on ourselves. When we unthinkingly change lanes in our car and cut someone else off, we let ourselves off the hook. We quickly dismiss the angry gesture emanating from the car behind us with the thought, *Lighten up! I'm sorry, for Pete's sake!* But let a person cut us off and almost cause an accident; we are not willing to extend the same graciousness to them as we are to ourselves. *Those stupid idiots!* we might think.

The IRS received the following note: "Gentlemen: Enclosed you will find a check for $150. I cheated on my income tax return last year and have not been able to sleep ever since. If I still have trouble sleeping I will send you the rest."[1] This man was willing to be honest up to a point . . . just enough to help him sleep. We minimize those areas of our life that continuously thwart us by duping ourselves into thinking that with a little more effort we will stop this time. As long as the struggles in our Christian growth remain locked inside our spirit and known only to God, then patterns or strongholds of besetting sin will defeat us.

The size of a triad says that this is going to be intimate. Self-disclosure increases in direct proportion to the trust we sense with our discipleship partners. Our histories will cause some of us to be reticent while others are more naturally trusting. A generation ago John Powell wrote a little book with the provocative title *Why Am I Afraid to Tell You Who I Am?* His answer: "Because if I tell you who I am, you may not like who I am, and it's all that I have."[2] Fear of personal rejection or condemnation lurks inside of us all. To the extent that we can find a safe place to be who we are, then we are free to discover that unique creation waiting to be fully unleashed.

What are the elements of transparent trust that will allow us to move gradually into the deep waters of transformation?

- Affirming one another through encouragement

- Walking with one another through difficult times

- Being a reflective listener who assists another to hear God's guidance in life's complexities

- Confessing our sins to one another that we may be healed

AFFIRMATION THROUGH ENCOURAGEMENT

The apostle Paul in his letter to the Colossians captures the overall tone that discipling relationships are intended to foster. "As God's chosen ones, holy and beloved, clothe yourselves with compassion, kindness, humility, meekness, and patience. Bear with one another and, if anyone has a complaint against another, forgive each other; just as the Lord has forgiven you, so you also must forgive. Above all, clothe yourselves with love, which binds everything together in perfect harmony" (Colossians 3:12-14). In essence, the people with whom we share the discipleship journey need to convey the attitude of unqualified desire that we be all that God intended us to be, primarily through the affirmation of our uniqueness and value to the Lord. Jesus began his public ministry with this affirmation by his Father: "You are my Son, marked and chosen by my love, pride of my life" (Mark 1:11 The Message). This is the same message that we need to convey to one another.

Gordon McDonald in *Restoring Your Spiritual Passion* comments on the cleansing and purifying power of rebuke by saying, "One solid and loving rebuke is worth a hundred affirmations."[3] I have often turned the intent of that statement around and focused on the affirmations by saying, "A hundred affirmations for every rebuke is just about the right ratio." The problem is that most of us are not living with a hundred words of encouragement to every word of correction. Prior to entering the sanctuary for public worship one Sunday, I ducked into the restroom. Standing side by side at the sink was one of the soloists who often performs, as well as participates, in worship leadership with our worship band. I took the opportunity to say, "Chris, I just want to thank you for the way you bless us in worship. When you sing it is obvious that it is to the Lord, and your singing takes me to the place of praise where I need to be. The Lord bless you for what you do for us as a worshiping community." You would have thought that I told him he had won the lottery. With emotion he said, "Thank you sooooo much. You have just made my day!"

We are starving for honest and meaningful affirmation in a world that knows better how to beat us up than build us up. In the intimacy of a triad we have the opportunity to observe the formation of the unique creations God has made each other to be and to affirm what God is birthing.

WALKING WITH EACH OTHER IN DIFFICULT TIMES

When you enter a covenantal relationship where you will stay together for a year or longer, you will have the opportunity to address life's highs and lows. Paul captures the rhythm of relationships in the body: "If one member suffers, all suffer together with it; if one member is honored, all rejoice together with it" (1 Corinthians 12:26). This is especially true in a triad. The nature of life is that there are circumstances over which we have no control, and these circumstances can have a devastating impact upon us. One of the privileges of this intimate relationship is to be able walk with one another during these times. Paul encourages the Thessalonians with these words: "Night and day we pray most earnestly that we may see you face to face and restore whatever is lacking in your faith" (1 Thessalonians 3:10). We gain trust through the faithfulness of partners who sustain us when the bottom has fallen out.

Previously I mentioned Mike, who had considerable financial woes because a commercial real estate deal had gone awry. Deferred taxes on the foreclosure of an office building left him with combined federal and state tax bills amounting to over a quarter of a million dollars. Mike was forced to sell his home, take out the equity and move his wife and five children to a less expensive location. Our weekly discipleship meetings came with updates on the latest legal strategies being deployed, the state of hopefulness of resolution and thoughts about how we might be of assistance. Mike's precarious position afforded us the opportunity to arrange a low-interest loan through members of the church to allow him to pay a portion of the taxes. A major lesson of discipleship that can be learned only in Christian community is the belief that God is good even when the circumstances of life would lead us to believe otherwise.

As I look back at my discipleship triads over the last decade and a half, every one of them had some quality of life-threatening circumstance touch at least one of the members of the triad. I have mentioned previously Ken's bout with cancer. I am convinced that our prayers and support for him during the heavy regimen of chemotherapy not only lengthened Ken's life way beyond the doctors' prognostication but also raised Ken up as a radiant witness to the love of Christ. I will always be deeply appreciative for the support I received when my parents died a month apart from each other. The voice mail from my group offering their love and encouragement brings warmth to my heart and a smile to my face even as I write these words. Then there's Frank who went to work clueless, thinking it was like any other day at the office. On arrival he was told to clear out his desk; this day would be his last. How does a man in the Silicon Valley survive such a blow? This is a place that equates work and self-esteem. We had the chance to catch Frank in his freefall before he hit bottom and then speak God's love into his life. Today Frank runs his own computer systems consulting business as a service not only to his customers but to the glory of God as well.

Being carried by the faith of others is often the way to learn to trust God. I have often said to people whose lives have come crashing down, "Let my faith carry you for a while. Some day you will be in a position to return the favor." This is exactly what a discipleship group can do as it builds toward transparent trust.

BEING A REFLECTIVE LISTENER

Scott is a high school art teacher who loves to coach football on the side. True, this is not your usual combination. When I invited Scott to join a triad, he was still reeling from the sting of having been released as the frosh-soph coach of the high school football team by an apparently jealous and threatened athletic director. Scott's teams had gone undefeated, while the varsity team was not faring as well under the athletic director. As I listened to Scott share his pain about this dismissal, it was obvious that there was a hole in his heart. He was wired to invest in kids as a coach. This was God's call upon his life. Yet Scott was trying to do the balancing act that all busy and capable people must do. He was married with three children ranging from the teens to infancy. He was also a conscientious teacher whose job never ends. In addition, he had been asked to serve as an elder at the church where I pastored. This was a role for which Scott was eminently qualified, and I drooled at the possibility of having him on my team.

Yet there was something obviously missing in Scott's life. Scott was torn between the shoulds of his life and this call to coach. He missed the opportunity to influence and disciple his team members toward godly character and to work for goals that only could be accomplished together. The athletic director, now a little more mature and secure, had seen his error and asked Scott again to become the frosh-soph football coach. Scott was reluctant. He wasn't sure he wanted to set himself up to be hurt again. Time would not permit Scott to be an elder in the church and the coach of a football team. The should from the church was clashing with the call of God. What a joy it was for me to help Scott see how God had wired Scott to serve him. The call of God on Scott was to invest in the lives of these teens and their families at this crucial juncture of their journey. The call to be an elder could wait. This was an unusual direction for me, the senior pastor of the church, to be steering Scott. Sheer self-interest said that I would love to have a man of Scott's ability and godly character as a partner in church leadership. Yet in our triad the responsibility was to help Scott become aware of the hand of God upon his life. He chose coaching.

There are a myriad of choices in our life that need to be sorted through to hear God's voice. God's voice can be drowned out by the din of the world or the confusion that comes from a multitude of choices. There is no end to issues where there is need for guidance from the Lord: direction in employment, ethical dilemmas in the workplace, bumps in marital relationships, an errant teen, unsaved family members or neighbors, discernment of God's call or passions of the heart. How we need places to sort out these conundrums with people who will stay with us and care long enough to follow through! This moves us out of the shallow end into the deeper waters of transparent trust.

Confessing Sin and Addressing the Addictions of the Heart

The deep end of the pool of transparent trust is the water of mutual confession of sin and addiction. To get to the deep end we must go through the shallower waters of encouragement, support through life's difficulties and prayerful listening. Only then are we likely to confess our patterns of besetting sin to one another.

My experience tells me that few believers have either the regular habit or the safe context in which to reveal to another human being what lurks in the recesses of our hearts. Until we get to the point where we can articulate to another those things that have a hold on us, we will live under the tyranny of our suppressed darkness. James admonished his readers, "Confess your sins to one another, and pray for one another, so that you may be healed" (James 5:16). James makes a direct connection between confession and healing. In this context, healing appears to be of a physical nature. Yet James believed that the health of one's spirit directly affects the health of one's body. Much bodily affliction is the result of spiritual or emotional sickness. If transformation into Christlikeness is related to being free from the darkness that can drag us down, then confession is a necessary means to free us from the bondage to sin and addiction.

What is the connection between confession and freedom? Bringing the shame of our guilt into the light before trusted members of the body of Christ can have a liberating effect. Once something is admitted before others, it begins to lose its power to control. Sin flourishes in the darkness, but its power dissipates in the light. In one of my triads, Sam signaled that he had something that he needed to entrust to the two of us. His halting voice and avoidance of eye contact, coupled with his nervous and self-conscious demeanor, said that a confession was coming. Sam told us that he had a longstanding obsession with pornography that was governing his life and affecting his marriage. As his partners on this journey toward wholeness, we assured him of our support and affirmed his courage as he tackled this problem. He stated his intent to join a twelve-step group of others struggling with sexual addiction and his desire to reveal this pattern to his wife. The relief in Sam was palpable. To be known and yet still loved was liberating. Admission of powerlessness in a strange way begins to reduce the power of darkness. In subsequent weeks we received reports of his commitment to a twelve-step program and the encouraging response of his wife to this struggle. Sam's boldness became an invitation to us all to go deeper and to withhold nothing that would get in the way of our obedience to Christ.

Martin Luther said that confession "is useful, even necessary, and I would not have it abolished. Indeed, I rejoice that it exists in the church of Christ, for it is a cure without equal for distressed consciences. For when we have laid bare our consciences to a brother and privately made known to him the evil that lurks within, we receive from our brother's lips the word of comfort spoken by God Himself. And if we accept this in faith, we find peace in the mercy of God speaking to us through our brother."[4]

Mutual confession is a major missing ingredient today in the process of Christlike transformation. To the extent that we live among fellow believers with a conscious awareness that we are living a double life, we will not have fellowship with each other or with God. This is the apostle John's point in his first letter. "If we say that we have fellowship with him while we are walking in darkness, we lie and do not do what is true; but if we walk in the light as he himself is in the light, we have fellowship with one another, and the blood of Jesus his Son cleanses us from all sin" (1 John 1:6-7). To the extent that we try to hide our sin before God, we are cut off to others in the body of Christ. Conversely, to the extent that we are willing to acknowledge those patterns or habits of sin to trusted, covenantal partners, then we will have fellowship with God.

To learn to swim in the deep waters of transparent trust is a necessary element for accelerated growth in the Christian life. Learning to swim can be a scary experience. But once you learn to trust the water to hold you up, you can relax and experience its refreshment. Relational transparency is the first necessary condition for transformation.

CLIMATIC CONDITION TWO:
THE TRUTH OF GOD'S WORD

The second of three environmental elements that create the conditions for accelerated growth is the truth of God's Word. Why is this? There is no better summary of the nature and the value of the Word of God than Paul's statement to his son in the faith, Timothy: "All scripture is inspired by God and is useful for teaching, for reproof, for correction, and for training in righteousness, so that everyone who belongs to God may be proficient, equipped for every good work" (2 Timothy 3:16-17).

The Scriptures of the Old and New Testament are unique among written documents. In them we fully hear God's word to us. In no other place can we find the complete story of God's self-revelation. Literally this God-breathed document is the plumb line of truth about God, ourselves and all matters of faith and practice. Paul tells us that it is useful for four things: teaching, reproof, correction and training in righteousness.

TEACHING

The word for teaching here can mean either to extend the hand of acceptance, such as cause to accept (persuasive), or to hand down (pass on). It is most likely this second nuance that Paul has in mind. Paul desires that Timothy feast on a body of knowledge, or a set tradition, which we generally refer to as doctrine. But Paul has in mind far more than head knowledge. He means a new reality that interprets the way things are. Larry Richards has given the best summary of the purpose of Scripture I have ever read: "In the word of God, the Spirit of God has revealed the true nature of the world we live in, the true nature of man and of God, the ultimate consummation of history, the pattern of relationships and responses to God and to life which corresponds with *the way things really are*."

It is particularly important in our day that a disciple has the opportunity to cover the essential teachings of the Christian life in a systematic and sequential fashion as a means of cultivating this new reality. We live at a time when the average person has little memory of the Christian faith. *The Tonight Show* with Jay Leno is an unlikely place to find evidence for this loss of memory, but one night Leno, microphone in hand, took to the streets asking people questions about their biblical knowledge. He approached two college-age women with the question, "Can you name one of the Ten Commandments?" Quizzical and blank looks led to this reply: "Freedom of speech?" Then Leno turned to a young man. "Who according to the Bible was eaten by a whale?" With confidence and excitement, the young man blurted out, "I know, I know, Pinocchio!"

For Christian leaders this means that we cannot assume that people have a reservoir of biblical knowledge. In fact, most potential disciples have bits and pieces of Christian teaching interspersed with worldviews from contemporary culture. This usually means that people have disconnected pieces of knowledge, much like puzzle pieces, but people have never put the pieces together to see the big picture of the Christian life. One of the participants in a discipling triad that I led was a woman about ten years my senior who had been reared in the home of a Congregational pastor. After we had completed our time together, she said to me, "Greg, I have a confession to make. When you asked me to join this group, I didn't think I had a whole lot to learn. After all, I had been studying the Scriptures all of my life, having been reared in a home where the Bible was central. But I discovered as we covered the faith in a systematic and sequential fashion that my understanding was much like a mosaic. I had clusters of tiles with a lot of empty spaces in between. This approach has allowed me to fill in all those places where tiles belong. I can now see in a much more comprehensive fashion how the Christian faith makes sense of it all." The Scripture is profitable for teaching.

REPROOF

First, the Scripture as body of teaching gives us the set of glasses through which to view reality. Then, this results in the ability to see the changes that we need to make in our lives. Literally the word *reproof* means to show someone his or her sin or summon the person to repentance. Scripture acts as the mirror to show us our true self over against the self we are being called to be. It is as if we look in a mirror of the Word and see two images side by side. One image is the way we are currently, whereas the second image is the way God intends us to be in Christ. The Scripture projects these contrasting images on the screen of our mind. In those moments when we clearly see the contrast between who we are and who we are to be, the Scripture acts with incisive conviction, like a stiletto piercing our soul. That conviction leads us to repentance and the desire to change.

A Christian couple decided during the season of Advent to take their four sons to different churches to introduce them the various forms of worship and Christmas traditions. One Sunday the family settled into the last row of a beautiful stone church flooded by the red and blue hues shining through the stained glass. They had observed the processions, anthems and the liturgy in full regalia, and then it came time for the sermon. The preacher of the morning stated his belief that God had probably asked many different women to receive the Christ child into their womb but had been turned down. So when Gabriel found Mary and she said yes, he was quite pleased, said the preacher. The youngest of the four boys, who has few unexpressed thoughts, blurted out so loudly that the last person in the distant choir could not have missed the declaration, "Where's he find *that* in the Bible?" Even this young one had a well-developed truth detector based upon the Scripture and therefore could offer a word of reproof.

CORRECTION

Reproof, though, is not meant to leave us wallowing in guilt and self-condemnation. In fact, the true conviction of the Holy Spirit leads immediately to the forgiving mercy of God. To the woman caught in adultery, Jesus said, "Neither do I condemn you. Go your way, and from now on do not sin again" (John 8:11). Jesus did not minimize her sin by pretending it was less than it was. Yet it did not lead to condemnation but to mercy. "Neither do I condemn you." True repentance leads to the sweetness of God's cleansing mercy. This is then followed by correction. Correction means to be restored or reestablished. If reproof is the rebuke of the Spirit that exposes, then correction means to be set straight or put back on the right path.

TRAINING IN RIGHTEOUSNESS

Once we are on the right path, we want to stay there. Literally the phrase "training in righteousness" means "training unto righteousness." The end goal of the Scripture is to guide and provide the inner power that would lead us to a godly life. The word *training* comes from the root "to train a child." This is reminiscent of Proverbs 22:6: "Train children in the right way, and when old, they will not stray." The Scripture is the training manual for righteous living.

John Ortberg reminds us that there is a huge difference between trying and training in the Christian life. Trying is attempting to do something without preparation. Too many supposed followers of Jesus are operating under a trying versus training paradigm. One would never try to run a marathon. Completing a marathon requires training. In preparation one would build stamina and endurance incrementally over time, while controlling one's diet and rest patterns. Ortberg observes, "The need for preparation, or training, does not stop when it comes to learning the art of forgiveness, or joy, or courage. In other words, it applies to a healthy and vibrant spiritual life just as it does to physical and intellectual activity. Learning to think, feel, and act like Jesus is at least as demanding as learning to run a marathon or play the piano."[5]

Training implies discipline. Any discipleship process will necessitate a disciplined practice of study, meditation and memorization of Scripture. Neil Cole has a variation on the triads described here. He calls them appropriately *Life Transformation Groups*.[6] One of the three disciplines for the group participants is the challenge to read twenty-five to thirty chapters of Scripture per week. In fact, those in the triad must report each week if they were able to complete the assigned reading. If anyone in the group was not able to complete the target amount, then they all have to read the same text again the next week. Cole wants participants to stretch and even to fail to complete the assignment so that they will have to repetitiously cover the material. By reading twenty-five to thirty chapters a week, an appetite for the Word of God is created. The Word is the seed of new life and must be deeply planted if it is to produce fruit. In *Discipleship Essentials* the study of Scripture is covered topically with Scripture memorization and biblical readings that follow a logical path to incrementally build the big picture of the Christian life.[7]

With study of the Word comes the practice of meditation and memorization. To meditate on Scripture is to allow the truth of God's Word to move from head to heart. It is to so dwell upon a truth that it becomes a part of our being. Someone has compared meditation with a cow chewing its cud. We want to turn the Word over and over again until it is digested. One of the ways to do this is through Scripture memorization. Scripture memorization has a number of benefits. We become what we place our minds on. Scripture says, "As a person thinks, so is he." Paul admonished the Romans to "be transformed by the renewing of your minds" (Romans 12:2).

Why is the mind the key to transformation? It is the mind that holds our beliefs, values, attitudes and perceptions. The process of growth in the Christian life is putting off beliefs and practices that are not honoring to God and replacing them with beliefs and practices that are. In Ephesians 4:25-32 Paul gives a number of illustrations of what can be called the principle of replacement or the "put off . . . put on" motif. For example, Ephesians 4:25 calls us to put away falsehood and put on truth; in Ephesians 4:28 thieves are told to give up stealing and instead find honest work. There is hardly a better way to assist the process of transforming our thinking and fulfilling the principle of replacement than to put our minds to the memorization of Scripture. Additionally, having Scripture at the ready can assist our ministry to fellow believers and undergird our witness to not-yet Christians.

In 2 Timothy 3:17 Paul draws his thought to a close about the source and value of Scripture by stating the goal is "that everyone who belongs to God may be proficient, equipped for every good work." The overall goal of discipleship is maturity, here defined as completeness. A means to that end is to immerse ourselves in Scripture in the context of transparent intimacy. This context then provides the internal power to do "every good work." As a friend of mine says, "The Word of God not only informs, it performs." The Word is God's *dynamis;* therefore it carries within it the power to carry out its intent. This is why Jesus equates the Word with the seed of new life. It is our responsibility to plant that seed deep within our lives so that the life within the Word can sprout and bear fruit.

CLIMATIC CONDITION THREE: MUTUAL ACCOUNTABILITY

The third environmental element that will contribute to creating just the right climatic conditions for accelerated growth is mutual accountability. In other words, the relationship between those on the discipleship journey together is covenantal. What is a covenant? A covenant is a written, mutual agreement between two or more parties that clearly states the expectations and commitments in the relationship. Implied in this definition is that the covenantal partners are giving each other authority to hold them to the covenant to which they have mutually agreed. Accountability has then been defined as "a willing decision to abide by certain standards and a voluntary submission of oneself to a review by others in which one's performance is evaluated in light of these standards."

Here is the rub. To willingly give others authority to hold us accountable is for most westerners a violation of what we hold most dear. I referenced earlier Robert Bellah's groundbreaking book *Habits of the Heart.* He found that freedom from obligation defined the core of what it is be to an American. Reared as we have been with the spirit of radical independence, almost everything in us rebels against mutual submission. We want to keep our own counsel. We want to be in control of our own choices, life direction, character formation, schedules.

Accountability brings us back to the core of what it means to be a disciple of Jesus. A disciple is one under authority. A disciple of Jesus is one who does not leave any doubt that it is Jesus who is exerting the formative influence over our lives. Jesus said, "If any want to become my followers, let them deny themselves and take up their cross daily and follow me" (Luke 9:23). The way to get serious about this truth is to practice coming under authority in our covenantal relationships in Christ.

Why a covenant? First, a covenant, complete with clear standards of mutual submission, empowers the leader of the triad to carry out his or her primary role: to be the keeper of the covenant. If there are no explicit, mutually agreed upon commitments, then the group leader is left without any basis to hold people accountable. Without a covenant, all leaders possess is their subjective understanding of what is entailed in the relationship.

Second, covenantal standards raise the level of intensity by setting the high bar of discipleship. One of the failings in the church is that we do not ask people to step up to what Jesus asked. Covenantal discipleship relationships can help us get serious about following Jesus on his terms.

Third, with a covenantal arrangement we invite our partners to hold us accountable. Positive peer pressure leads us to follow through. If we have Scriptures to memorize that must be recited to one another, or if we have committed to put into practice a scriptural command, the chances of our following through are greatly enhanced when we have to give account to our partners.

Fourth, a clear covenant at the outset forces the prospective member of a triad to assess whether he or she has what it takes to be in a discipling relationship. Reviewing the covenant is part of the initial invitation to the journey together. It is a sobering moment to examine whether one has the time, the energy and the commitment to do what is necessary to engage in a discipleship relationship.

As an illustration of a covenant of mutual accountability, the following is the suggested covenant included in *Discipleship Essentials*. This covenant is what I talk through with someone as I am inviting him or her into the discipleship triad. My commentary is in brackets.

A Disciple's Covenant

In order to grow toward maturity in Christ and complete *Discipleship Essentials*, I commit myself to the following standards:

1. Complete all assignments on a weekly basis prior to my discipleship appointment in order to contribute fully. *[I generally say that it will take approximately two hours per week to complete all four parts of the assignment, plus a variable amount of time to memorize the Scripture.]*

2. Meet weekly with my discipleship partners for approximately one and one-half hours to dialogue over the content of the assignments. *[To this point, the minimum time commitment is three and a half hours per week, plus travel time to the location where the triad meets.]*

3. Offer myself fully to the Lord with the anticipation that I am entering a time of accelerated transformation during this discipleship period. *[I want people to expect that the process of growth will have a hothouse effect.]*

4. Contribute to a climate of honesty, trust and personal vulnerability in a spirit of mutual upbuilding. *[I state that this will be perhaps the most honest and self-revealing Christian relationship they have experienced, and that it will lead to mutual confession. I often ask, "How do you feel about that?" The conflicting feelings of fear and attraction are common.]*

5. Give serious consideration to continuing the discipling chain by committing myself to invest in at least two other people for the year following the initial completion of *Discipleship Essentials*. *[A part of the upfront agenda is that the disciple is not only growing to maturity in Christ but also being equipped to disciple others. Yet the phrase "give serious consideration to" is used in deference to "I will continue the discipling chain," because the person entering the relationship has, as yet, not experienced a discipling relationship. You can't commit yourself to something you have yet to experience, but you can plant the expectation from the outset.]*

THE DISCIPLESHIP DIFFERENCE

What sets the triad off from other discipling relationships that contribute to maturity? Why does this context more than others create an accelerated environment for growth? Perhaps figure 8.1 shows it best.

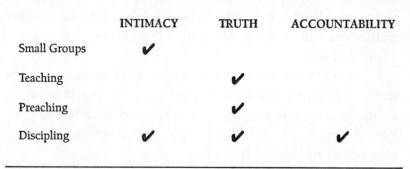

	INTIMACY	TRUTH	ACCOUNTABILITY
Small Groups	✔		
Teaching		✔	
Preaching		✔	
Discipling	✔	✔	✔

Figure 8.1. Power of the discipling model

I have clear recollections of when the insights contained in this chart were revealed. One of the necessary steps to complete the requirements for my doctor of ministry degree was to invite my faculty supervisor, Dr. Roberta Hestenes,[8] to come to the church campus to meet with those who walked with me in this discipleship experiment. As you may recall, the focus of my project was to implement in three contexts a discipleship curriculum I had written: one-on-one, a small group of ten and a triad. The role of the faculty supervisor was to debrief those who had helped me shape the project and to tease out the discoveries from the different contexts. About ten of us gathered around the conference room table with the white board behind Dr. Hestenes. Being more than a bit nervous with how the discussion would go, I was delighted with the feedback and the reported impact on the lives, especially of those in the smaller discipleship units. As Dr. Hestenes listened and delighted in their report, she saw the power of these discipling units. With excitement she sprang to her feet and drew figure 8.1 (p. 171) on the white board.

She said a small group of six to ten people tends to emphasize fellowship or intimacy, while truth and accountability are secondary. In classroom teaching or preaching within public worship, truth content is primary, with intimacy and accountability taking a back seat. What makes the discipling context transformative, she said, is that it brings all of these elements together in a balanced way.

Every believer or inquirer must be given the opportunity to be invited into a relationship of intimate trust that provides the opportunity to explore and apply God's Word within a setting of relational motivation, and finally, make a sober commitment to a covenant of accountability.

What would happen to the health of your ministry five to seven years from now if multiplying discipleship groups proliferated in the church community? Celebration Life Ministries in Elk Grove, California, was founded in 1997 with "reproducing and discipleship at the very core of our identity as a church," says Pastor Mike DeRuyter. Mike tells their story:

In late 1997 we began Celebration Life Ministries as "pioneering work" without any existing core group to launch our ministry. Our core was literally created a few at a time. During the early phases of building our foundation, there were several immediate issues that we knew we would have to deal with: 1. No trained, mature leadership. 2. Few common faith assumptions/ little common faith language. Our core was either unchurched or from a dizzying array of denominational backgrounds. 3. A large percentage of damaged and needy people.

My wife and I spent the majority of our ministry time during the early stages of our plant facilitating discipleship groups. We used *Discipleship Essentials* in the triad format, with an emphasis on group reproduction. I met with the men; my wife met with the women. We were able to build relationships and do the pastoral work called for by deeply wounded people. We began to build a common language as a church. Agenda harmony was positively impacted. And we have a tool that allowed newer/younger Christians to become leaders/facilitators in a relatively short time (about six months). Today, all of our elders and deacons are discipleship group graduates. Additionally, the majority of our ministry leaders are discipleship group graduates/participants or leaders. In fact, the trend is that new ministry emerges out of the discipleship groups themselves.

Can you see what this careful approach to growing disciples would do for the health of the church or ministry? Can you visualize the impact of multiplication over three to five to seven years? I have watched the effect these multiplying discipleship groups have on a church. Over time the church culture is so transformed that a new consensus has developed. The new standard to which people aspire is to become self-initiating, reproducing, fully devoted followers of Jesus.

THE HINGE

I began chapter six with the image of a hinge. The church, I said, is like a nonfunctioning door because it leans against the biblical door frame of the call to disciple making. The hinge that connects the door to the door frame is a practical strategy. The necessary elements in a church-based strategy to make reproducing disciples are to establish a relational disciple-making process that is rooted in a reproducible model (triads) that brings together the transformative elements of life change.

In chapter nine I fasten the last hinge to connect the door (the church) to the door frame (biblical vision): the implementation steps to create a multiplying network of discipleship triads.

9

PRACTICALITIES OF
DISCIPLE MAKING

Have you ever had the nagging feeling that there is something in your life that you are supposed to do, but you don't have a model or picture in your mind of what to do? We know that we are to leave a legacy of changed lives. Yet it remains an unattainable ideal, because we don't have a practical strategy to make it a reality. We want to be able to say what Paul said about those who would come after us, "You yourselves are our letter, written on our hearts, to be known and read by all; and you show that you are a letter of Christ, prepared by us, written not with ink but with the Spirit of the living God, not on tablets of stone but on tablets of human hearts" (2 Corinthians 3:2-3). I continue to be moved by the phrase in the letter from Jane (pp. 132-33), who wrote, "I feel like I am the fruit of your fruit! And praise the Lord more fruit is being produced!" I know that this is the only thing that matters. How do we go about seeing the creation of living epistles in the form of self-initiating, reproducing, fully devoted followers of Jesus?

My hope is that through this book you have been given a means to leave a legacy. For many it is not a matter of motivation but know-how. We lack a working model of how to take the approach of Jesus and Paul and make it a reality in ministry and church life. In this closing chapter I intend to be as practical as possible and leave nothing to the imagination.

Our agenda in this chapter is to address the following practical questions:

- What is a workable disciple-making model?

- Who should we invite into the discipling process?

- How do we get started?

- How can we grow a multigenerational network of disciples?

- How do we keep up the motivation for multiplication through the generations?

A WORKABLE DISCIPLE-MAKING MODEL

Let me make explicit what has been implicit. The model of disciple making I propose is one person inviting two others into a covenantal relationship structured around a Bible-based curriculum. For approximately a year they meet weekly for about an hour and a half per session, which then reproduces unto the next generation.

When I was in college, Corrie ten Boom, the great Dutch Christian and survivor of Nazi German prison camps, spoke to our group. I don't have a clear recollection of the question I asked her, but I have a clear recollection of her response. I suppose I was trying to impress my peers with some deeply profound query. She stopped me in my tracks. "K.I.S.S.," she said. "Keep it simple, stupid." What I propose may sound insultingly simple. Yet it has been my experience that if our ministry schemes are overly complex, they will either never get off the ground or will eventually collapse under their own administrative weight.

Here is how it works: Invest in a relationship with two others for give or take a year. (A discipling relationship varies in length because of the relational dynamics and the growth processes unique to each relationship.) Then multiply. Each person invites two others for the next leg of the journey and does it all again. Same content, different relationships. People have asked me, "Won't this get boring covering the same content repetitiously?" My standard reply from experience is a resounding "No!" Why? The relational dynamics are always different, and this difference keeps the process interesting. People are wonderfully unique. Each triad will have its own life or personality because the people will make it interesting. If you are the initiator of the discipling relationship, you also will be at another stage of development. Let the network grow organically. Multiplication begets multiplication. And in three to five to seven years, you will be able to look back at the family tree and see that the branches have stretched to five or six generations. The joy will come when you see names of people in the family, three or four generations removed from you, that can be traced back to your initial triad (see figure 9.1, p. 178, for an example).

WHO IS INVITED?

You are ready to take the plunge and experiment with a discipleship triad. But how do you discern whom you should approach? Remember that a distinguishing dynamic of a discipling relationship that varies from other mentoring relationships[1] is that the discipler issues the call. Following Jesus' example, it is vital that we issue a call to the journey of discipleship. This means that the invitation to discipleship should be preceded by a period of prayerful discernment. It is vital to have a settled conviction that the Lord is drawing us to those to whom we are issuing this invitation.

What criteria should we use to guide our prayer for those who would join us on the discipleship journey? We should look for the same qualities in people that Jesus spotted in the Twelve or that Paul urged Timothy to observe when entrusting the gospel to the

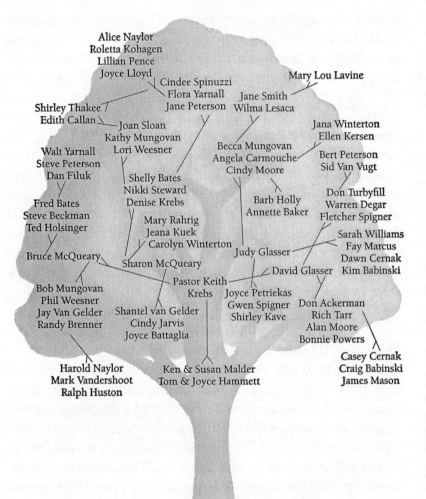

Figure 9.1. The "family tree" of a discipler

next generation: faithfulness, reliability or dependability (2 Timothy 2:2).

Jesus did not seem to be in a hurry to name the Twelve. As we observed, perhaps six months transpired from the commencement of his public ministry until he publicly identified those who would be his apostles. His selection of the Twelve followed a night in prayer. His entire ministry rested on the quality of people that he chose. If you are going to invest a year or more of your time with two others with the intent of multiplying, whom you invite is of paramount importance. What were the qualities Jesus looked for in those he called, and how do these qualities serve as a guide for us? I would propose two primary qualities as determinative: loyalty and teachability.

Loyalty. Jesus had a wonderful sense of humor. The day that Jesus made Peter the most successful fisherman he had ever been was the day Jesus called him away from his trade. After Peter had been fishing all night, having caught nothing and having cleaned and hung his nets up to dry, Jesus asked him to go fishing again. With reluctance, while probably muttering under his breath something like, "What does a rabbi know about fishing?" Peter dropped his net into the sea, only to haul in the largest catch of his life. No fish story Peter had ever heard or told around the campfire came close to this incident. It was against the backdrop of smashing triumph that Jesus said to Peter and the others, "From now on, you will be catching people" (Luke 5:10). Peter and the others left their means of support, families and familiar surroundings to meander from village to village, following this renegade carpenter. What Jesus sought in his followers was loyalty to him above all else.

Though we may not be called away from our places of employment and families on an itinerant, apostolic ministry to follow Jesus, what Jesus still seeks in his followers is that we value him above all else. This is evidenced by a willingness to bring our behavior and lifestyle in alignment with Jesus' desires, an openness to self-examination and a hunger to place our lives at his disposal. Our prayer might be, "Lord, give me eyes to see, and draw my heart to those who have a deep desire to be all that you want them to be. May that be true of me also."

Teachability. Jesus chose the disciples for what they would become, not for what they were at the time of their call. We noted in chapter four that the disciples seemed to have none of the characteristics that would distinguish them according to the world's standards. None held key positions of influence. They were not drawn from the respected religious ranks, such as the Levitical priesthood or the religious Supreme Court, the Sanhedrin. They had not acquired the equivalent of a Ph.D. that would give them academic credentials. They fit Paul's description of the Corinthians: "Not many of you were wise by human standards, not many were powerful, not many were of noble birth" (1 Corinthians 1:26).

This should serve as a caution. There is a temptation to base our selection on what might distinguish people according to cultural norms. Leaders in the church are often selected because of natural leadership ability, an outgoing personality, membership in a respected profession, reputation, positions of influence or wealth. Jesus' thought was, "Give me teachable, loyal people, and watch me change the world." There is almost the sense that the less one has invested in the world, the more available one would be to him. We can easily overlook a disciple who has great potential because he or she does not match the world's value system.

In my first professional ministry with college students, it was often the quiet, shy and indistinguishable who became the most focused, influential disciples of Jesus by the time they became juniors and seniors in college. In Jane Smith's letter to me eight years after her graduation from the University of Pittsburgh, she referenced three names of students who were most influential in her life. I had the privilege of close association with the two men and one woman. When they arrived as freshmen at the university, they were naturally reticent and, by personality, not standouts. Yet there was a desire in them to follow the adventurous life to which Jesus called them. They grew into self-initiating, reproducing followers of Jesus. By contrast, it was often the most self-assured, outgoing, attractive personalities who were not willing to pay the price of discipleship. They naturally gravitated to visible leadership because they fed on the accolades of the crowd, but behind the scenes they were not willing to discipline themselves for the privilege of leadership.

What a remarkable thing it is to recall that Jesus literally turned the world upside down with fishermen, a tax collector and a terrorist (religious zealot). Never underestimate what can be done with loyal and teachable people. Teachability is a hunger to learn and humility to not care from whom you learn it.

At the writing of this book, I am in a triad with a man is his early thirties. I was drawn to him because of his evident desire to know what God had designed him to do with his life. He was reading books on how to get in touch with the passions that God had placed in his heart. He made appointments with people he thought could help him discern his spiritual gift profile and aid in his discovery of call. He currently works as an engineer designing air conditioning systems. But he is drawn to children and wonders if he should be a teacher. He volunteers one night a week as a counselor with a program called Confident Kids and now takes one morning a week to act as a volunteer aide in a kindergarten classroom to explore whether this is God's vocational call on his life. He is a poster child for teachability.

The first step in creating a reproducible discipleship group is to find the right people. The right people are marked by a willingness to be loyal to Jesus and have a teachable spirit. Simply ask the Lord to lay on your heart those in whom he is already at work. Keep a journal. Write down the names of people the Lord seems to bring to mind. Continue to pray over them until there is a settled conviction that the Holy Spirit is tying your lives together.

HOW TO START

The following step-by-step guide can serve as a blueprint to follow when you are ready to approach people with the invitation to discipleship.

Make the invitation. State that as a result of prayer you feel drawn to invite the person to join you in a mutual journey of discipleship toward maturity in Christ. Stress that this is not a random invitation but comes as the fruit of prayer. It might be helpful to express that Jesus' model of making disciples was to have a few who were "with him" and that the way the Lord continues to make disciples is through intentional relationships. If *Discipleship Essentials* is your curriculum of choice, then it would be appropriate to look at its definition of *discipling* on page 17, so that the person has an idea of the kind of relationship this will be.

Review the discipleship curriculum. Walk through an overview of the table of contents and the layout of one of the lessons so that the disciplee gets a sense for what is involved. I would also stress the fact that discipling is not about completing a lesson in a workbook. The curriculum is a tool that provides some structure for the relationship. Tools do not make disciples. The Lord uses people to make disciples. The tool raises the issues of discipleship, but the discipler incarnates the principles and convictions in a life.

Review the covenant line by line. Review "A Disciple's Covenant" from page 14 of *Discipleship Essentials* (or whatever covenant you may be using as a basis for accountability). It is imperative that the disciplee has the opportunity to ponder the extent of commitment involved in the relationship. This has to do with time expectations (approximately five hours a week of preparation and meeting time, and whatever travel is involved with getting to the meeting place), relational risk and life change. You want to raise the question implicitly: Are you ready to consider serious change in any area of your life? From the outset you are raising the bar and calling a person to step up to it.

Ask the person to prayerfully consider this relationship over the next week. Do not seek or allow an immediate response to the invitation to join a triad. You want the person to consider the time commitment in light of the larger configuration of life's responsibilities and to make the adjustments in schedule, if necessary, to make this relationship work. In addition, you want a person to ruminate over internal readiness, which usually means facing the fear of what might be ahead. I would be very concerned if a potential disciple did not have some fear or concern about keeping the commitment. It is the weight of the commitment that you want to be processed.

Inform the person that a third person will be joining you in the triad. If you have not settled on or do not already have a third person in mind, enlist this person's support in helping discern who that third person should be.

Set the meeting time of your first gathering. At the first meeting of the discipleship group, ask each person, yourself included, to share the process they went through in making the commitment to this group. Were there any adjustments to schedule that had to be made? Were there inner impediments that had to be faced? I like to have a covenant signing ceremony as the first meeting. In each other's presence you sign the covenant as an open demonstration of everyone's commitment to keep the covenant and as an invitation to be held accountable to it by each other. Note that there will be a couple of opportunities to review and renew the covenant in *Discipleship Essentials* (pp. 80, 146). These are essentially opportunities for self-evaluation against the covenantal standards, as well as chances to reflect on your level of satisfaction with the triad experience to date. Each person enters with specific expectations as to what the relationship will be. It is important for each to be able to share disappointments, if there have been any, and make course corrections. The time of review also serves as an opportunity to celebrate the benefits while in process. It is important that the two invitees know that a major role of the triad convener is to be a keeper of the covenant. The leader is there to help the members complete what they say they are committed to accomplish.

Guide the participants through the sessions. In an hour and a half session I would allow about thirty minutes for personal sharing, follow-up from previous sessions, mutual enjoyment of what is happening in each other's lives, and prayer. The other hour is spent on the responses to the questions in the material that each person has previously prepared. Go at a pace that seems comfortable to the group and is not so regimented that it does not allow time to chase rabbit trails. You want to encourage participants to introduce questions that are prompted from the study. It is also important not to rush the personal application to the various dimensions of one's life. In *Discipleship Essentials,* questions have been carefully crafted to bring the truth home to the lives of discipleship partners.

The convener of the triad completes all the lessons. This person also fully participates in the discussions with his or her insights as one of the participating members of the group. The format is so simple that leadership is easily transferable. After an initial number of sessions in which the leader has had a chance to model the time distribution and interactive format, encourage a rotation of leadership. The primary role of the leader is to guide the opening sharing and walk the group through the lesson material that is already laid out. Rotating leadership of the sessions has the value in allowing each person to gain the confidence that he or she could lead such a group in the future.

The discipler models transparency. This person shares personal struggles, prayer concerns and confession of sin. The group will probably go as deep personally as, or take risks to the extent that, they see the leader doing. But trust develops incrementally. The degree of self-revelation will need to be matched to the level of trust that has been developed. In addition, the disciplers need not feel that they have all the answers to biblical and theological questions that are raised. Feel free to say, "I don't know, but I will find out," or "Why don't we each seek answers to that question this week and come back to share our insights." Discipleship is in part about taking responsibility and initiative to search out the truth.

GROWING A MULTIGENERATIONAL NETWORK OF DISCIPLES

We now move from the focus on a single triad to the fulfillment of a vision that there will be a multiplication of self-initiating, reproducing followers of Jesus. We visualize cell reproduction, where the DNA from an initial cell replicates itself in adjoining cells (see figure 9.2). How do we lay the foundations for this kind of reproduction?

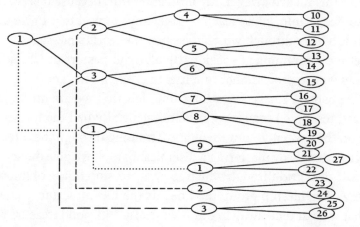

Figure 9.2. Multiplication

Almost everything I say in this section will put the brakes on our attempt to speed up the process of replication.

Start with one triad. My advice to those who are just starting to experience the dynamics of this type of discipleship relationship is to take a year and "just do it" (my apologies to Nike). Get a feel for what happens in a small discipleship group. Place the discipling partners high on your prayer list. Make regular intercession for them based upon the identified areas of needed growth. In addition, ask the Lord to show you what your disciplees could become under his shaping influence. Just as Jesus saw that Peter would be "the rock" when he was anything but, so ask the Lord to ignite your imagination to see the potential purpose and call that the Lord has on these lives.

If you are using a curriculum like *Discipleship Essentials,* it is helpful to master its content so that you have a lifetime discipleship tool at your disposal. Having gone through various versions of *Discipleship Essentials* over the last seventeen years, I can tell what is on each page of the material. Mention a page number and I can recite the content . . . almost. Yet I have found it enormously valuable to have this tucked away in my head and heart, because it serves as a resource to inform my teaching, fuel any counsel that I give and provide a filter through which to screen the world's messages.

Let me for a moment speak particularly to pastors or Christian leaders whose professional role it is to pass on "the good deposit of the gospel." I have for a long time felt that we are an underutilized resource because we have not generally had the means to pass on the content of our theological training through the filter of our experience. By mastering a discipleship tool, we give ourselves a theological grid through which to pass our storehouse of knowledge. A discipleship group provides us the incentive and context so that we can tuck away in our own hearts "the good treasure entrusted to you" (2 Timothy 1:14).

A multigenerational network of discipleship may seem to have meager beginnings if it starts with one discipleship triad. But you have to begin somewhere and get beyond the need to have a big splash that will lead to instantaneous change. Quick fixes have led to the discipleship morass we are in. Even though the need for discipling will run way ahead of your ability to meet it in the short run, remember that programs have failed to deliver the necessary life change over time. Leroy Eims a generation ago asked, "What then is the problem today? Why don't we see more of this [disciple making] going one? Why are fruitful, dedicated mature disciples so rare? The biggest reason is that all too often we have relied on programs or materials or some other thing to do the job. The ministry is carried on by people, not programs."[2]

Have a long-term vision. Jesus went about his ministry with a relaxed urgency. He never seemed to be in a hurry but always kept his eye laser focused on the destination. Jesus had a conscious awareness that he was a man born to die. Always looming ahead was this rendezvous with self-sacrifice. It was for "this hour" that he had come. Yet along the way he was training his disciples to carry on after he left. Jesus knew that the training program of the disciples would terminate with the completion of his mission in the cross. It would be their turn to carry on the mission. The baton had to be passed. Jesus never wavered from that vision.

How long do you have left in your ministry where you are? Will you be there three years . . . five years . . . seven years . . . longer? What do you want to leave behind? There is a saying in relationship to change: You never seem to accomplish as much as you want in the short run but can accomplish a lot more than you can imagine in the long run. Start building a network of disciple making. Fight every impulse in your being that says, "We must see results by next month or even in the next six months." Intentionally growing people takes time. You can't accomplish as much as you like in the short run, but you will be able to see far more than you can imagine in the long run.

One of the mistakes from which I was graciously rescued and taught hard lessons had to do with trying to rapidly multiply disciples. (Any time you hear people say that they have an approach to rapidly growing disciples, treat them as if they are used car salesmen. If anything sounds too good to be true, it probably is too good to be true.) In my first experiment with these triads, I had started and developed the network exclusively among men since I (a male) was the initiator of this ministry. Once the replication had occurred through a few triads, women in the congregation began clamoring for something similar. I had a brainstorm. I decided to issue an invitation to approximately fifteen highly regarded, spiritually mature women to come to a Saturday morning session where I would lay out for them the challenge and vision of disciple making. The Saturday morning arrived. I was deeply gratified that these quality people would take the time to hear the challenge I was to place before them. I gave what I thought was one of my best "win one for the Gipper" speeches. In order to provide the biblical imperative, I sketched out Jesus' approach to investing in a few. I affirmed that others in the congregation looked up to them as winsome followers of Jesus. The time for the "ask" had come. "I challenge you to find two other women who could join you in a journey of discipleship. You be their guides into deeper maturity in Christ so that we can develop this discipling network among women in our congregation as well."

Expecting that these women would storm the locker room door in order to take their places on the playing field, I was thoroughly deflated by their response. "Coach," they said, "we hate to tell you, but before we can play the game, we need to know the fundamentals. We have never experienced the kind of relationship you are describing. How can you expect us to lead people through something that we have never experienced? Why don't you slow down? Instead, you take two of us through what you have in mind. Lay the foundations solidly in their lives and build from there." I was trying to jump-start discipling among the women. I wanted to launch fifteen triads simultaneously. A perfect plan to rapidly grow disciples, I thought. I guess I was the used car salesman that day. I had visions of a transformed congregation within two years. They said, essentially, "Take a long-term view. Slow down. Do it right." And they were right.

A growing discipleship network is like yeast that slowly penetrates the dough, causing it to rise almost imperceptibly. In the first year with an initial triad, you have the satisfaction of watching intimacy develop and transformation occur. In the second year you encourage and coach into existence two new triads, plus start a third one of your own. In the third year, these three have become nine, and so on. It takes up to five years before critical mass has been reached. As I said before, it takes less than 20 percent of a congregation to set the pace for the rest. A small percentage of value holders determine what a church or ministry is all about. At the five-year mark there are so many stories of life change and so much buzz about what these triads have meant to those involved that people will beg for the opportunity to become a part of these groups.

I can hear it now. "Five years! I don't have five years!" Are you going to be there five years from now? Then what is it that you want to leave behind? If you are a pastor reading this book, do you want to measure your ministry by the number of sermons preached, worship services designed, homes visited, hospital calls made, counseling sessions held, or the number of self-initiating, reproducing, fully devoted followers of Jesus? I reiterate, we are in the predicament we are in with the church of Jesus Christ today because we do not have enough leaders who have enough vision to think small.

Let me remind you of Robert Coleman's challenge: "One must decide where he wants his ministry to count—in the momentary applause of popular recognition or in the reproduction of his life in a few chosen ones who will carry on his work after he has gone? Really, it is a question of which generation we are living for."

Select carefully and wisely. The key element in growing a multi-generational network of disciple making is to start with the right people. Just as a building is only as strong as its foundation, so whom you select to initiate the network will determine whether multiplication occurs.

Whom you initially select will vary depending on your discipling model and context of ministry. The primary setting I have had in mind throughout this book is the myriads of established churches that have had little to no intentional disciple making. If this describes your situation, then I would begin with the most well-grounded and respected followers of Jesus in your community. An added qualifier that comes with more than a touch of self-interest is that they should be stable members of your community. In other words, look for people who have a good chance of staying around for a while.

Why should you begin with those who to the rest of the community already appear to be fairly mature in the faith? First, they probably have not been discipled or taught to disciple others. The women about whom I wrote were highly regarded for their spiritual depth, but to a person they had never been intentionally discipled. You have a great opportunity to take those who have already demonstrated a heart for God and turn them into reproducers. Second, their reputations, for all the right reasons, will give credibility to this new discipling adventure. Third, you want to ensure, as much as you can, a return on your investment. When you spend approximately a year with two others, you want to know that this was worthwhile. You are trying to see people become self-initiating followers of Jesus but also adopt a lifestyle of reproduction. You are about growing disciple makers. Those who are well grounded and stable, who have already demonstrated that they are dependable, reliable and faithful, are your best bet for replication.

The previous paragraph was written primarily for those who are attempting to lead a church through renewal. For those of you who are fortunate enough to be in a setting where you have more people coming to Christ than you can keep up with, you have another challenge. You cannot wait five years, because you will be committing spiritual infanticide if you do. In this setting you must take a two-pronged approach simultaneously. You need to gather people in small groups (approximately ten) for fellowship and provide them with some spiritual grounding. It is much easier and quicker to grow small-group leaders who can create at the least a minimal nurturing environment. At the same time you must begin to do all that I said previously in regard to discipling and let the network grow. In five to seven years you will have produced enough disciplers for all the new converts, but in the meantime you must settle for larger nurturing, fellowship groups.

What if you are planting a church? This is the perfect time to make disciple making a part of the lifestyle of the congregation. A part of every staff person's job description is to have at least two others in whom they are investing on a regular basis. At the conclusion of chapter eight I shared the story of a church plant that was founded on a discipling practice and vision.

For an alternative discipling model from the one I have presented here, I again commend to you Neil Cole's *Life Transformation Groups*.[3] Cole focuses on a different target group. He uses these LTGs, as he calls them, as an evangelistic tool. His heart is to witness transformation in the lives of the most unlikely unbelievers. His LTGs meet in coffee houses where the tattooed, body pierced, and purple haired may be found. The future leaders in his ministry are those who have been called out of lifestyles in open rebellion against God to a transformed life in Jesus Christ.

Under this heading of selecting carefully and wisely, it is appropriate to identify my failings. In retrospect, the mistakes I have made in choosing discipling partners have usually occurred when others have approached me and asked if I would disciple them or if they could be in one of my triads. Why might this be ground for caution? First, it is very flattering to have people want to spend time with you. Second, it is hard to displease people. How do you say no to persons whose stated agenda is that they want to grow in Christ? For these two reasons, it is difficult to pray with objectivity about whether this person is God's call on your time. Since a necessary characteristic of disciple making is for the discipler to issue the call, in this situation the discipler is being asked to confirm someone else's request. But this is not the most serious reservation. Not only are the discipler's motives in question, but so is the one who has approached you. What is the person's reason for approaching you with the request to be in a triad with you?

My two most disastrous triad experiences came as a result of my responding to the invitation of others while not carefully examining the reasons they wanted to be with me. Here is the real issue. What is the reason for wanting to be in a discipling relationship? Is it primarily to grow into Christlikeness, or is there a hidden agenda?

In the first instance, being a new pastor at the church, I was approached by two men who stated that they wanted to provide support for me while I was getting my legs in this fledgling ministry. I was flattered and certainly in need. What was intended to be a support for me and a discipleship group for the three of us quickly became neither. From all that I could tell, these men appeared to be highly motivated disciples of Jesus. One had spent a number of years in a church-planting ministry in Europe, while the other had a reputation for entrepreneurial ministry as a businessman. What I didn't discern was that these were two disgruntled ex-elders who had moved to the margin of the church. Week after week I was bombarded with a litany of complaints about the current group of elders, the self-focused nature of the church, the style of worship, the lack of evangelism. After some months, I told them that their negative attitude was detrimental to my ability to lead the church that I was learning to love.

The second aborted triad also included a person who had approached me about wanting to spend some time with me. Sam was an outgoing and brash owner of his own small business. He and his family were high profile and deeply invested in the church's ministry. Their children were scattered throughout the youth program, and Sam's wife was the "mother" to half (or so it seemed) of the teenagers in the congregation. Sam was a salesman par excellence, and he sold me on his eagerness for this type of relationship. Problems began to show up fairly early on. Sam would come to our sessions with the weekly assignment only partially completed. He might arrive late or have some reason as to why he had to leave early. It was evident that he was not ready for this discipline, because ultimately he was not serious about integrating all of his life under the lordship of Christ.

A confrontation with Sam was precipitated after people from the congregation stated to me their surprise that Sam was a part of a discipleship group. These people were employees in Sam's business. In the workplace they saw a man whose demeanor was very different from the warm persona he displayed in church. According to them, his leadership style was that of a tyrant. His emotional outbursts caused everyone to walk on eggshells. I eventually had to ask Sam about the accuracy of this inconsistency between his church face and the face he presented elsewhere. A person who truly wanted to be a disciple of Jesus would have responded—if not initially, then eventually—in a spirit of repentance. He would have acknowledged his double life as contrary to Christ's desires and asked the group to help him live a consistent life for Christ's sake. Instead, he cut off the relationship because he was offended that I would raise such an issue.

Is there any sure way to know the heart of the person you are inviting to join you on this journey? None that I know of. But be appropriately cautious with those who seek you out to spend time with you. If you are a pastor or a prominent figure in the Christian community, you already know that people might vicariously gain a sense of self-importance through association. This is not the fertile soil out of which a disciple is made.

If you want to grow a multigenerational discipling network, start with one triad, have a long-term vision, and select carefully and wisely, especially at the foundational stage of establishing the network.

KEEPING THE MOTIVATION FOR MULTIPLICATION

Once the discipling network begins to multiply, a concern will naturally arise. How do you keep putting energy into the system once it moves away from the center of vision? To start anything of significance there must be a visionary who is energized to see it become a reality. This is true of discipling. The visionary sees the possibilities of a multigenerational network of disciple making. He or she is committed to making self-initiating, reproducing disciples of Jesus as a lifestyle, but once the initial groups have given birth, how can the vision for reproduction be sustained? In other words, how do you pastor a decentralized ministry?

One of the temptations to avoid is to solve this problem by turning discipling into a program and thereby killing this self-reproducing organism. In my previous pastorate we never made a public recruiting announcement about this discipleship ministry. Come September, when all church ministries resume, we didn't get up on a Sunday morning and announce an opportunity to be in a discipleship group along with the myriad of other ministries. We avoided putting the groups onto a synchronized schedule following the school calendar from September to June. Occasionally we might have participants in a triad share the life-changing benefits with the congregation in worship, retreats or other ministries. Even after the public witness we did not give people a ready-made way to get into a discipleship group. I wanted the hunger and intrigue to build. What I avoided was making this ministry into a program we had to sustain by building an administrative superstructure. The genius behind triads is that you can start them without having to run a gauntlet of committees and thereby having the idea talked to death by people who do not have a heart for what you are trying to accomplish. To sustain the triad network you need only a handful of people who want to see the network of relationship continue to multiply. The most people I have ever had tending to this network was three, and this was with well over 150 people active in the discipleship process.

What did these oversight groups do to sustain the vision and energy for multiplication? The following were some of the varied ways we experimented with energy infusion.

Periodically call together the discipling network as a whole for sharing, motivation and instruction. Occasionally we invited all the current participants in the triads together to cross-pollinate. Since an individual triad can feel isolated and disconnected, we were constantly looking for ways to help people feel a part of a movement. At these gatherings we would mix up the triad participants to form sharing groups. People would share with each other their reasons for responding to the invitation and the particular flavor of their group life. We usually would handpick two or three people to tell about the influence this experience had on their lives. An exhortation would be issued from Scripture to carry on the discipling chain to the next generation.

Invite a guest speaker. A variation is to invite in a speaker who is committed to disciple making and can speak with passion. One highlight was the privilege of having Dr. Keith Phillips from World Impact, Inc., address our burgeoning network. He had written *The Making of a Disciple* and had fully integrated a disciple-making strategy into the urban centers of the United States. Just having an outside voice say the same things you as a leader have been saying raises your credibility. A guest can often say things in a fresh way, using life-impacting stories out of their context that can reignite the vision of multiplication.

Meet with discipling leaders in groups of three or four. In between the larger group motivational settings, it is fruitful to bring together three or four triad conveners to process their experience together. One of the roles of those in your discipling oversight group could be to convene these smaller sessions. We found it invaluable for the leaders of the groups to share mutual experience, problem solve and gain ideas from each other as to how they were handling their time in their groups. This then became another opportunity to remind them to challenge their group members to reproduce.

Meet with those in the last third of their triad. Depending upon how thorough you want to be in knowing where the groups are on their discipleship journey, you might want to meet with those who are beyond the two-thirds mark in completing their discipleship curriculum. With *Discipleship Essentials* there is a trigger point built into the curriculum where the participants are to begin praying about and selecting those who will join them in the next leg of the journey. If you know that groups are approaching that point, a contact can be made to encourage them to follow this process. It is also helpful to know if and why people are reticent to reproduce.

Publish a discipling newsletter. In my last two churches we developed a periodic newsletter that went out to all the participants in the triads. We called the newsletter *Discipling Network News* (Southern California) and *Discipleship Bytes* (Silicon Valley). The purpose of the newsletter was primarily to help people feel that they were a part of a growing organism. Written testimonies of group participants served to encourage others. Articles on the biblical vision of discipling were a way to keep connecting people back to the initial impetus. Names were listed of all the participants in a triad to create the feel that God was up to something big.

In my experience this approach to disciple making has yielded approximately a 75 percent reproduction for at least one generation following the initial completion of a triad. A pastor's responsibilities in a given week can take one far afield from the people building business. No matter how crazy my week became, I knew that I had at least one opportunity in my weekly schedule to feel like I was fulfilling my pastoral call to make disciples of all nations.

LEAVING A LEGACY

One of the most deflating moments for the United States in the history of the Olympic games occurred in 1988 in Seoul, Korea. The American 4 x 100 relay team was poised to break the world record and assume its position as the best in the world. It had peerless athletes. There was no thought that this team could lose. The only question was whether they would crack the world record. Yet as the final leg of the race approached, the unthinkable happened. The Americans dropped the baton. The handoff was not completed. In an instant, the race was over. The crowd, electrified moments earlier, were left in stunned silence. The American team had arrogantly relied on their inherent speed and failed to sufficiently practice the handoff that was so crucial for the completion of the race.

"Every Christian must see themselves as the link to the next generation," writes William Barclay. We need to practice the handoff. When all else fails, read the directions. It is not that Jesus' way has been tried and found wanting; it has been largely talked about but not implemented. Return to small, reproducible, long-term relationships as the means of transmission of the gospel from one generation to the next.

Legacies are not about leaving large sums of money to our children or being immortalized by getting our names etched on a building. When we get to the shore's edge and know that there is a boat there waiting to take us to the other side to be with Jesus, all that will truly matter is the names of family, friends and others who are self initiating, reproducing, fully devoted followers of Jesus because we made it the priority of our lives to walk with them toward maturity in Christ. There is no better eternal investment or legacy to leave behind.

This sentiment is captured well in a poem by William Allen Dromgoole:

The Bridge Builder

An old man, going a lone highway,
Came at evening, cold and gray,
To a chasm, vast and deep and wide,
Through which was flowing a sullen tide.
The old man crossed the twilight dim—
That sullen stream had no fears for him;
But he turned, when he had reached the other side,
He built a bridge to span the tide.

"Old man," said a fellow pilgrim near,
"You are wasting strength building here.
Your journey will end with the ending day;
You never again will pass this way.
You have crossed the chasm, deep and wide,
Why build up the bridge at the eventide?"

The builder lifted his old gray head.
"Good friend, in the path I have come," he said.
"There followeth after me today
A youth whose feet must pass this way.
This chasm that has been naught to me
To that fair-haired youth may be a pitfall be.
He, too, must cross in the twilight dim;
Good friend, I am building the bridge for him."

APPENDIX
Frequently Asked Questions

Should the genders be kept separate or mixed in a discipleship re-lationship?

Some people might argue that true relational maturity ultimately is the ability of the sexes to understand their differences, but I would argue that in the intimacy of a triad it is best to have same-sex groups. Having led a group with two women and groups with married couples, I have found it difficult to be transparent about particular male struggles with women present. My guess is that the same would be true of women with men. The other concern is the obvious inappropriate bonding that could occur in a cross-sex group of this intimate a nature. It has been well documented historically that in an intense spiritual environment heart wires can get crossed. Spiritual passion can easily cross over to sexual passion.

Why is a triad or quadrad the right size for a discipleship group? Why is a group of ten not just as effective?

I identified three ingredients that converge to make for the transformational environment: relational transparency, the truth of God's Word and life-change accountability. The small number maximizes the interactive nature of these three ingredients. More people water down the impact of these three elements. Relational transparency built upon trust takes longer and becomes more difficult the more people involved. The opportunities to interact over and share insights into God's Word are decreased with greater numbers. With a greater number of people there is a natural tendency to move away from life-change accountability to measuring accountability by external standards and commitments.

What does the leader do if a participant is not following through on the covenant?

One of the reasons for and necessities of a covenant is to empower the leader. Without an explicit covenant the leader has no means for accountability. Having a written covenant, which serves as a basis for recruiting and convening the triad, will minimize this difficulty. It also places in the hands of the leader a tool that can be used to call those who have agreed to the covenant back to their stated commitments. In *Discipleship Essentials* there are two built-in opportunities to review and renew the covenant. This process is laid out so that the participants self-assess. People tend to be harder on themselves than their partners might be. Depending on where he or she is in relation to the review of the covenant, a leader might want to wait until the group has an opportunity to self-assess and recommit to the covenant. If the problem seems more urgent, then it would be appropriate for the leader to ask for one-on-one time with a member of the triad. I would propose a question such as "It appears that you are having difficulty with [whatever the observed behavior]. Is that right? Is there a way I can be of help?" If the problem continues after offered assistance, then the leader will have to make the hard call and say, "It appears that this is not the right time for you to be in this kind of relationship."

How can we encourage those who are lagging in some aspect of preparation?

This is where the leader can be a model and a coach. For example, I often hear complaints about how difficult it is to memorize Scripture. Some people will use the excuse of age. They say, "I just can't remember things like I used to." Besides not letting them off the hook, you might want to explore some coaching techniques. Putting verses on three-by-five cards and carrying them in your purse or pocket for consistent review can be helpful. Go over suggested ways to prepare the material in the lesson. It is better to take twenty to thirty minutes a day and cover material in bite-size chunks than to cram it all in the night before the group gathers. Talk together as a group about the means and patterns each of you use to get ready for the time together. Keeping a life-change journal can be useful. Record changes in habits, thinking patterns, life direction, understanding of God, or relationships that have come as a result of the discipleship process. This can serve as a wonderful record of the way the Lord is in the process of "making all things new."

Is it necessary that church leaders be on board for a discipleship network to be successful?

If the long-term desire is to have a culture-shaping effect on the life of a church or ministry, the leaders must share the philosophy and lifestyle approach to discipling. The ultimate goal would be that the ministry staff and the decision-making leaders would not only adopt the philosophy of discipling but also engage in the practice of people building. That having been said, if you as an individual have a vision for making disciples that is not yet shared by church leaders, that should not stop you from beginning your engagement in disciple making. This can be a quiet ministry that grows within the body. In order not to sow seeds of dissension, I would either seek permission from the pastor(s) or church board, or at the least make them aware of your intention. This then lays the groundwork for a bottom-up change and states your desire to work in concert with church leaders.

What if church leaders have a different approach or structure in place?

Some ministry approaches are antithetical to each other and therefore cannot coexist. This leads us back to the underlying values and philosophy of ministry. Fundamentally, triads are based upon a belief that there are three necessary ingredients that make for transformation. Triads are a means to this deeper end. Transformation or making disciples is not necessarily the intent and practice of many ministries. If the fundamental values are not shared, then the ability to create the conditions necessary for transformation will become unattainable.

NOTES

Introduction: A Story of Transformation

[1]This curriculum, after years of experimentation, refinement and self-publication, has become *Discipleship Essentials* (Downers Grove, Ill.: InterVarsity Press, 1998). Some readers may remember the self-published version, *A Disciple's Guide for Today*. A doctor of ministry degree is for people who are in professional ministry and want to remain there while continuing their education.

[2]Bill Hull, *The Disciple Making Pastor* (Grand Rapids, Mich.: Revell, 1988), p. 14.

[3]Over the last century there has been no shortage of excellent resources that focus on the pattern of disciple making. See A. B. Bruce, *The Training of the Twelve* (Grand Rapids, Mich.: Kregel, 1971); Robert Coleman, *The Master Plan of Evangelism* (Old Tappan, N.J.: Revell, 1963); William Hendriksen, *Disciples Are Made, Not Born* (Colorado Springs: Chariot Victor, 1983); Leroy Eims, *The Lost Art of Disciple Making* (Colorado Springs, Colo.: NavPress, 1978).

Chapter 1: The Discipleship Gap

[1]Max De Pree, *Leadership Is an Art* (New York: Bantam Doubleday Dell, 1989), p. 11.

[2]The Eastbourne Consultation, *Joint Statement on Discipleship*, September 24, 1999.

[3]John R. W. Stott, quoted as a participating member of the Eastbourne Consultation.

[4]Barna's working definition of born-again Christians is persons who have "made a personal commitment to Jesus Christ that is still important today" and are assured that they will go to heaven because they have "confessed their sins and accepted Christ as Savior."

[5]Barna Research Online, "Born-Again Christians," research archives <www.barna.org>.

[6]The Gallup Organization, Religion, "Would you describe yourself as 'born-again' or evangelical?" <www.gallup.com>.

[7]Interview with Cal Thomas, *Christianity Today*, April 25, 1994.

[8]George Barna, *Growing True Disciples* (Ventura, Calif.: Issachar Resources, 2000), p. 62.

[9]The verb *gymnazō* ("train") is the root of the English word *gymnasium*.

[10]Barna Research Online, "More Than Twenty Million Church Adults Actively Involved in Spiritual Growth Efforts," May 9, 2000 <www.barna.org>.

[11]Barna, *Growing True Disciples*, p. 2.

[12]Ibid., p. 11.

[13]Dallas Willard, *The Divine Conspiracy* (San Francisco: Harper, 1998), p. 315.

[14]Martin Luther, *Three Treatises: An Open Letter to the German Nobility* (Philadelphia: Fortress, 1960), pp. 14-17.

[15]Os Guinness, *The Gravedigger File* (Downers Grove, Ill.: InterVarsity Press, 1983), p. 169.

[16]George Barna, quoted in Bill Hull, *The Disciple Making Pastor* (Grand Rapids, Mich.: Revell, 1988), p. 21.

[17]Ray Stedman, *Body Life* (Glendale, Calif.: Regal, 1972), p. 37.

[18]George Gallup Jr. and Jim Castelli, *The People's Religion* (New York: Macmillan, 1989), p. 60.

[19]Alec Gallup and Wendy W. Simmons, The Gallup Organization, poll releases, October 20, 2000.

[20]Barna Research Online, "American Bible Knowledge Is in the Ballpark but Often Off Base," July 12, 2000 <www.barna.org>.

[21]Barna, *Growing True Disciples*, p. 52.

[22]Ibid.

[23]Bill Hybels, The Contagious Evangelism Conference, Willow Creek Community Church, October 16-18, 2000.

[24]Joel Barker, *Future Edge: Discovering the New Paradigms of Success* (New York: William Morrow, 1992), p. 147.

[25]John P. Kotter, *Leading Change* (Boston: Harvard Business School Press, 1996), p. 35.

[26]Barna Research Online, "Barna Addresses Four Top Ministry Issues of Church Leaders," September 25, 2000 <www.barna.org>.

Chapter 2: The Discipleship Malaise

[1]Greg Ogden, *Unfinished Business: Returning the Ministry to the People of God* (Grand Rapids, Mich.: Zondervan, 2003). The book was originally published under the title *The New Reformation*. It has been revised and re-released by Zondervan.

[2]Ibid., chap. 6.

[3]Rick Warren, *The Purpose-Driven Church* (Grand Rapids, Mich.: Zondervan, 1995), p. 382.

[4]George Barna, *Making True Disciples* (Ventura, Calif.: Issachar Resources, 2000), p. 79.

[5]Ibid.

[6]Ibid.

[7]Dallas Willard, *The Divine Conspiracy* (San Francisco: Harper, 1998), p. 40.

[8]Ibid., p. xv.

[9]Ibid., p. 315.

[10]Michael Wilkins, *Following the Master: A Biblical Theology of Discipleship* (Grand Rapids, Mich.: Zondervan, 1992), p. 25.

[11]Dwight Pentecost, quoted in ibid., p. 14.

[12]Wade Clark Roof and William McKinney, *American Mainline Religion: Its Changing Shape and Future* (New Brunswick, N.J.: Rutgers University Press, 1987), pp. 18-19.

[13]Warren, *Purpose-Driven Church,* p. 109.

[14]Barna, *Growing True Disciples,* p. 41.

[15]The Eastbourne Consultation, *Joint Statement on Discipleship,* September 24, 1999.

[16]Barna, *Growing True Disciples,* p. 42.

[17]George Orwell, quoted in Bill Hull, *The Disciple Making Pastor* (Grand Rapids, Mich.: Revell, 1988), p. 13.

Chapter 3: Why Jesus Invested in a Few

[1]A. B. Bruce, *The Training of the Twelve* (Grand Rapids, Mich.: Kregel, 1971), p. 11.

[2]Gerhard Kittel, *Theological Dictionary of the New Testament,* ed. and trans. Geoffrey Bromiley, 10 vols. (Grand Rapids, Mich.: Eerdmans, 1967), 4:441.

[3]Lawrence Richards, *Christian Education: Seeking to Become Like Jesus* (Grand Rapids, Mich.: Zondervan, 1975), p. 83. Social scientists have identified three stages of social influence that lead to in-depth attitude change. The most superficial change occurs through compliance. A person conforms or changes because an authority has control over the individual. The second level is imitation, which is the desire to conform because one wants to be like another person. This moves to identification, when there is some emotional involvement with the other person. Finally, internalization means that adopted attitudes and behavior have become intrinsically rewarding.

[4]Alicia Britt Chole, "Purposeful Proximity—Jesus' Model of Mentoring," *Enrichment Journal: A Journal of Pentecostal Ministry* (spring 2001) <www.ag.org/enrichmentjournal/2001102/062_proximity.cfm>.

[5]Bruce, *Training of the Twelve,* p. 13.

[6]Leroy Eims, *The Lost Art of Disciple Making* (Colorado Springs, Colo.: NavPress, 1978), p. 45.

[7]Bruce, *Training of the Twelve,* p. 13.

[8]Paul M. Zehr and Jim Egli, *Alternative Models of Mennonite Pastoral Formation*

(Elkhart, Ind.: Institute of Mennonite Studies, 1992), p. 43.

[9]Eugene Peterson, *Traveling Light* (Downers Grove, Ill.: InterVarsity Press, 1982), p. 182.

[10]Robert Coleman, *The Master Plan of Evangelism* (Old Tappan, N.J.: Revell, 1963), p. 21.

[11]George Martin, quoted in David Watson, *Called and Committed* (Wheaton, Ill.: Harold Shaw, 1982), p. 53.

[12]Coleman, *Master Plan of Evangelism*, p. 21.

Chapter 4: Jesus' Preparatory Empowerment Model

[1]Robert Coleman, *The Master Plan of Evangelism* (Old Tappan, N.J.: Revell, 1963), p. 117.

[2]David Watson, *Called and Committed* (Wheaton, Ill.: Harold Shaw, 1982), p. 9.

[3]Leighton Ford, *Transforming Leadership* (Downers Grove, Ill.: InterVarsity Press, 1991), p. 200.

[4]Servant Quarters <www.servant.org/pa_m.htm>.

[5]A. B. Bruce, *The Training of the Twelve* (Grand Rapids, Mich.: Kregel, 1971), p. 14.

[6]Ibid.

[7]Martin Luther King Jr., quoted in John Claypool, *Opening Blind Eyes* (Nashville: Abingdon, 1983), p. 75.

[8]Michael Wilkins, *Following the Master: A Biblical Theology of Discipleship* (Grand Rapids, Mich.: Zondervan, 1992), p. 107.

[9]Paul Hersey and Ken Blanchard, *Situational Leadership: A Summary* (Escondido, Calif.: Center for Leadership Studies, 2000), p. 2.

[10]Thomas Schirrmacher, "Jesus as Master Educator" <www.visi.com/~m/ab/schirrmacher/educator.html>.

[11]Coleman, *Master Plan of Evangelism*, p. 39.

[12]Ibid., p. 38.

[13]B. Gerhardsson, *The Origins of the Gospel Tradition* (Philadelphia: Fortress, 1979), p. 17.

[14]Jesus was not denying that he is good or humbly refusing to receive such a designation. Jesus' retort was meant to call up short the rich young ruler's casual use of the term *good,* for only God is good.

[15]Coleman, *Master Plan of Evangelism*, p. 110.

[16]Ibid., p. 112.

Chapter 5: Paul's Empowerment Model

[1]There is only one reference to Paul having disciples, but this is not Paul's self-designation. "They [Paul's enemies] were watching the gates day and night so

that they might kill him; but his disciples took him by night and let him down through an opening in the wall, lowering him in a basket" (Acts 9:24-25).

[2]Jack O. Balswick and Judith K. Balswick, *The Family: A Christian Perspective on the Contemporary Home* (Grand Rapids, Mich.: Baker, 1991), p. 94.

[3]Ibid., p. 108.

[4]Ibid., p. 105.

[5]Quoted in Linda L. Belleville, *Patterns of Discipleship in the New Testament* (Grand Rapids, Mich.: Eerdmans, 1996), p. 121.

[6]C. S. Lewis, *Mere Christianity* (New York: Macmillan, 1952), p. 189.

[7]L. Douglas DeNike and Norman Tiber, "Neurotic Behavior," *Foundations of Abnormal Psychology* (New York: Holt, Rinehart and Winston, 1968), p. 355.

[8]Bill Hull, *The Disciple Making Pastor* (Grand Rapids, Mich.: Revell, 1988), p. 91.

[9]Elton Trueblood, *The Incendiary Fellowship* (New York: Harper & Row, 1967), p. 43.

[10]Balswick and Balswick, *Family*, p. 107.

[11]Ibid.

Chapter 6: Life Investment

[1]Frank Tillapaugh, *The Church Unleashed* (Ventura, Calif.: Regal Books, 1982), p. 71.

[2]Greg Ogden, *Discipleship Essentials: A Guide to Building Your Life in Christ* (Downers Grove, Ill.: InterVarsity Press, 1998).

[3]Alicia Britt Chole, "Purposeful Proximity—Jesus' Model of Mentoring," *Enrichment Journal: A Journal of Pentecostal Ministry* (spring 2001) <www.ag.org/enrichmentjournal/2001102/062_proximity.cfm>.

[4]Paul D. Stanley and J. Robert Clinton, *Connecting: The Mentoring Relationships You Need to Succeed in Life* (Colorado Springs, Colo.: NavPress, 1992), p. 167.

[5]Dick Wolden, quoted in *Discipleship Bytes,* the discipleship newsletter of Saratoga Federated Church, Saratoga, California (April 1996).

[6]Robert Coleman, *The Master Plan of Evangelism* (Old Tappan, N.J.: Revell, 1963), p. 37.

[7]Bill Hull, *The Disciple-Making Church* (Grand Rapids, Mich.: Revell, 1988), p. 32.

[8]International Leaders for Discipleship <www.cookministries.com>, emphasis added.

[9]Ogden, *Discipleship Essentials*, p. 17.

[10]Michael Wilkins, *Following the Master: A Biblical Theology of Discipleship* (Grand Rapids, Mich.: Zondervan, 1992), p. 44.

[11]Stanley and Clinton, *Connecting*, p. 48.

[12]Keith Philips, *The Making of a Disciple* (Old Tappan, N.J.: Revell, 1981), p. 15.

[13]Howard Snyder, *Liberating the Church* (Downers Grove, Ill.: InterVarsity Press, 1983), p. 248.

Chapter 7: Multiplication

[1]Gary W. Kuhne, "Follow-up—An Overview," in *Discipleship: The Best Writing from the Most Experienced Disciple Makers* (Grand Rapids, Mich.: Zondervan, 1981), p. 117.

[2]Ibid.

[3]Paul D. Stanley and J. Robert Clinton, *Connecting: The Mentoring Relationships You Need to Succeed in Life* (Colorado Springs, Colo.: NavPress, 1992), p. 48.

[4]Keith Phillips, *The Making of a Disciple* (Old Tappan, N.J.: Revell, 1981), p. 15.

[5]Stanley and Clinton, *Connecting*, p. 65.

[6]Ibid.

[7]Ibid., p. 73.

[8]Ibid., p. 124.

Chapter 8: Transformation

[1]Charles Swindoll, *Come Before Winter* (Portland, Ore.: Multnomah, 1985), p. 91.

[2]John Powell, *Why Am I Afraid to Tell You Who I Am?* (reprint, Allen, Tex.: Thomas More, 1995).

[3]Gordon McDonald, *Restoring Your Spiritual Passion* (Nashville: Thomas Nelson, 1985), p. 191.

[4]Martin Luther, quoted in Keith Miller, *Sin: Overcoming the Ultimate Deadly Addiction* (San Francisco: Harper & Row, 1987), p. 29.

[5]John Ortberg, *The Life You've Always Wanted* (Grand Rapids, Mich.: Zondervan, 1997), p. 48.

[6]Neil Cole, *Cultivating a Life for God* (Carol Stream, Ill.: Church Smart Resources, 1999). Three disciplines are practiced within Life Transformation Groups: reading twenty-five to thirty chapters of Scripture a week; confession sharing around Character Conversation Questions; Strategic Prayer Focus, which is praying that unbelieving friends will come to Christ.

[7]Ogden, *Discipleship Essentials*, p. 1. The twenty-four lessons are divided into four categories: Growing Up in Christ (beginning to practice basic spiritual disciplines); Understanding the Message of Christ (comprehending the core teaching about the nature of God and the person, work and benefits of Christ); Becoming Like Christ (the process and qualities of transformation by the Holy Spirit); Serving Christ (engaging in Christ's ministry).

[8]At the time Dr. Hestenes was associate professor of Christian formation and discipleship at Fuller Theological Seminary.

Chapter 9: Practicalities of Disciple Making

[1]See chapter seven for the working definitions of spiritual guide, coach and sponsor.

[2]Leroy Eims, *The Lost Art of Disciple Making* (Colorado Springs, Colo.: NavPress, 1978), p. 45.

[3]Neil Cole, *Cultivating a Life for God* (Carol Stream, Ill.: Church Smart Resources, 1999).